PENGUIN BOOKS

FLOYD ON SPAIN

Keith Floyd was born in 1943 and educated at Wellington School, Somerset. Since then he has devoted his life to cooking, except for a few brief excursions into the Army, antiques and the wine trade. Happily released from the rigours of running a restaurant by a chance meeting with a television producer, he has presented a number of highly successful television cookery series, of which *Floyd on Spain* is the most recent, and written several bestselling books, of which Penguin also publishes *Floyd on Oz*. When he is not hurtling around the world he spends his time in Devon, where he owns a pub.

FLOYD ON SPAIN

KEITH FLOYD

PENGUIN BOOKS

PENGUIN BOOKS

Published by the Penguin Group
Penguin Books Ltd, 27 Wrights Lane, London W8 5TZ, England
Penguin Books USA Inc., 375 Hudson Street, New York, New York 10014, USA
Penguin Books Australia Ltd, Ringwood, Victoria, Australia
Penguin Books Canada Ltd, 10 Alcorn Avenue, Toronto, Ontario, Canada M4V 3B2
Penguin Books (NZ) Ltd, 182–190 Wairau Road, Auckland 10, New Zealand

Penguin Books Ltd, Registered Offices: Harmondsworth, Middlesex, England

First published by Michael Joseph Ltd 1992
Published in Penguin Books 1993
1 3 5 7 9 10 8 6 4 2

Recipe photographer: Laurie Evans
Home economist: Berit Vinegrad
Stylist: Leslie Richardson
Cookery adviser: Sue Ashworth
Illustrator: Jane Brewster

Printed in England by Clays Ltd, St Ives plc

Contents

INTRODUCTION

In the backroom of a Bristol dockside bar frequented by donkey-jacketed wharfmen, languid duffel-coated art students and corduroy-jacketed advertising executives, who dreamt of writing a play or novel but who spent more time drawing faces on the thick froth of their stout, I hung out on the fringe of a folk-music-cum-poetry-writing, quasi-beatnik society.

We sat on wooden benches in the back, shiny, cream-painted room with concrete floor and listened to such diverse people as a Jewish folk duo called the Havarine, a raucous red-bearded giant called Noel Murphy, an Irish folk singer, even indeed to Dominic Behan, Brendan's brother, reciting his turgid poems.

During those halycon days of the early 1960s, ten shillings in Bristol would buy you a bus ticket into town, a few pints, entrance to the folk club and a spaghetti bolognaise in one of the newly-invented trattorias. Stout was still imported by ship from Dublin, and young actors like Peter O'Toole, and other alumni of the Bristol Old Vic, were occasionally spotted.

It was at the folk club I met a thin, bespectacled, balding young man who turned out to be seventeen but whom I took to be at least thirty. He said he was a poet and related to a former president of the United States. He spoke with passion and excitement of his plans to go to Ibiza, an idyllic island, he explained, off the coast of Spain. The Mediterranean country where wine, art and happiness flowed like honey from the big black candy mountain.

Intrigued by his apparent knowledge, by his tales of Goya, Velázquez and Cervantes, his admiration for Robert Graves who found inspiration from the island of Majorca, his understanding of Spain and his devout attendance at the Tatler continental cinema in Old Market, Bristol, where obscure and esoteric films were screened, I accepted an invitation to have a drink at his home after the folk club had finished.

Would his mother mind, I asked, our going back at 11 o'clock at night?

We left the poets and artists, the denizens of the smoke-filled club, and roared off on a Vespa 125 scooter to high suburbia, Westbury-on-Trym, Bristol. There, cross-legged on the floor sipping Rocamar, the cultural life-blood of the early 1960s, he sat silent like a Buddhist monk as Maria Callas played on his veneered mahogany gramophone (in stark contrast to the Little Richard and Buddy Holly I played on my Dansette in my small bedroom at my parents' house). Periodically he gave me a recitation on the possible joys of living in Ibiza, questioned me about Jean Genet, urged me to read Sartre's *Iron in the Soul*, dismissed Jack Kerouac as an American bum, and expounded that only through opera, Maria Callas and Spain could one achieve eternal happiness.

I was pondering on all these imponderables when his mother, a tea-planter's wife from Calcutta, entered the room rather like Lady Bracknell and ordered me imperiously home. David was asleep in a puddle of Rocamar. As I left in embarrassment I promised to meet him at the Tatler to see a Buñuel film, something he said would epitomise the golden glory and the dark power that was Spain.

The first time I had heard about Spain had been while studying for my 'O' level in 1958, when the prescribed book had been *The Gun* by C.S. Forester, set in Spain during the Napoleonic Wars.

But the novel was best known to us fifteen-year-olds because of page 77 on which the French general, Marshal Joffré, is in bed with a woman and there is a reference to a piece of her naked flesh, a possible thigh and the hint of a breast. Even so, bizarre as it may be, this book set me on to a vicarious interest in Spain and through Orwell, Laurie Lee and Hemingway I developed a passion for the place and, of course, an intense curiosity about the food and wines. Hemingway described some mouth-watering meals in dark tavernas and happy times on pavement bars. I wanted to see for myself.

But as a cub reporter earning £4 7s 6d a week with a Vespa to run I had little chance of realising that particular dream.

Circumstances and times changed and in the 1970s I found myself a (totally self-deceiving) restaurateur and after a minor hiccup, that is, a divorce and the liquidation of my business, I found myself living on a boat off the Mediterranean coast of Spain, eating grilled *gambas* and sardines, wondering how on earth I could survive. But survive I did mainly by cooking, washing up in restaurants or, along with my erstwhile friend Hector Gordon, acting either as crew, English teachers, chauffeurs, or companions to wealthy Scandinavians (all of this will be revealed in full detail in my amusing forthcoming autobiography). But often my existence was perilous and ephemeral and I didn't have the chance to find the Spain of Hemingway or Laurie Lee.

Fade to black. I have not seen David Taft for twenty years or Hector Gordon for fifteen and I am in Spain with a film crew, money and letters of introduction. At last a dream realised, to search out and enjoy the food and drink of Spain. Rocamar has gone, it no longer exists, no bad thing. Franco has gone, no bad thing. Tourism is being reshaped, a very good thing.

In the few months I spent filming there I managed to separate the food of the medallioned Mafia of gilt-edged coastal Spain from the bubbling, passionate core of what is Spanish gastronomy. Apart from the time, care and love that is devoted to this cooking, the slow simmering reductions of onions and tomatoes, the thickening of stews with Moorish *picadas*, the sizzling excitement of fresh fish barbecuing over vine root embers, apart from the power and glory real or imagined – what sets Spanish cuisine apart from the others is that it is 'Happy Food'. And this book, really a hastily concocted sketch of what could be a masterpiece, is dedicated to 'Happy Food'. It is just a little selection from the huge number of dishes that appealed to me: speak to Goya or Velázquez about the greater canvas.

PS Apart from the people I met in Spain who were so helpful, this book is dedicated to David Taft and Hector Gordon – and Miguel Sierra Sanchez of Torremolinos who said, 'You can only make a good *gazpacho* if you use happy tomatoes.'

Think about it.

Keith Floyd, Tuckenhay, 1992

Basic Sauces, Relishes and Stocks

Mayonnaise

Mayonesa

Makes 660ml (just over 1 pint)

4 large egg yolks
Salt
White pepper – freshly ground, if possible
2 tablespoons lemon juice or white wine vinegar
1 teaspoon cayenne pepper or mustard powder
600ml (1 pint) olive oil

Home-made mayonnaise is a cinch to make and tastes far superior to anything that comes in a jar. A good tip is to make sure that everything is at (warm) room temperature before you start – not only the ingredients, but the bowl and whisk as well.

First, plop the egg yolks into a large warmed bowl and mix them up with a few shakes of salt and pepper. Stir in the lemon juice or vinegar and the cayenne or mustard. Now add the oil, drop by drop to begin with, stirring all the time with a whisk or a wooden spoon.

As the mayonnaise emulsifies (that is, doesn't look separated) you can add the oil in a slow drizzle, stirring all the time until the oil is used up. Taste it, and add a little more salt and pepper if you need to.

Alternatively, you could put all the ingredients, apart from the oil, into a food processor or blender and then slowly drizzle in the oil as they whizz round. It takes seconds. Because this mayonnaise uses fresh egg yolks, you must store it in the fridge and use within 3–4 days. Make less if you can't use it all so quickly.

Garlic Mayonnaise

Alioli

This is brilliant, for example, with prawns, hard-boiled eggs, or cold chicken but my wife likes to dip her chips into it.

Makes 280ml (almost 1/2 pint)

4 cloves of garlic, peeled
2 egg yolks
Pinch of salt
Shake of white pepper
250ml (8fl oz) olive oil

To make this by hand, crush the garlic really well until completely pulverised. You can do this with a large pestle and mortar, or on a chopping board, scrunching the garlic cloves down with the flat part of a large cook's knife; then put them into a large bowl.

Add the egg yolks, salt and pepper and stir to combine. Now, using a hand whisk, stir the egg mixture continuously, while you add the olive oil, drop by drop to begin with, then gradually building up to a slow drizzle, until you have a wonderful thick garlic mayonnaise. Taste and adjust the seasoning, if necessary.

You can make this in a food processor or blender instead, if you wish. Start off by whizzing together the garlic, egg yolks and seasoning, adding the oil in a slow drizzle as the motor is running.

Tomato Sauce

Salsa de Tomate

Makes 450ml (3/4 pint)

4 tablespoons olive oil
1 medium onion, finely chopped
4 cloves of garlic, crushed
675g (1 1/2 lb) ripe tomatoes, skinned and roughly chopped
1 tablespoon white sugar
2 tablespoons raspberry vinegar
1 tablespoon chopped fresh parsley
1 tablespoon chopped fresh basil
300ml (1/2 pint) cold water
Salt
Freshly ground black pepper

Heat the oil in a saucepan and throw in the onion and garlic. Fry these together for about 5 minutes over a medium heat until they have softened, but don't let them brown.

Tip all the other ingredients into the pan, heat gently and simmer for at least half an hour. Leave off the lid so that the liquid reduces and the flavour concentrates. Check the seasoning, adding a few shakes of salt and pepper if you need to.

Romesco Sauce

Salsa Romesca

Some uses of this sauce: cold as a useful dip for raw vegetables (*crudités*) or tortilla chips or hot with fried eggs or deep-fried chicken wings. A useful party sauce.

Makes 600ml (1 pint)

1 large sweet red pepper, seeded and chopped or, even better,
2 'New Mexico' dried red peppers or Spanish ñoras, *see page 204*
2 hot dried red chilli peppers, seeded
250ml (8fl oz) olive oil
2 thin slices of French bread
225g (8oz) tomatoes, skinned and chopped
4 cloves of garlic, finely chopped
25g (1oz) ground almonds
125ml (4fl oz) red wine vinegar
Salt
Freshly ground black pepper

If you are using the elongated 'New Mexico' dried peppers or the Spanish *ñoras*, soak them in warm water with the chilli peppers for about half an hour until they are soft. Drain, dry and chop them.

Heat 4 tablespoons of the oil in a frying pan, pop in the slices of French bread and fry until golden on both sides. Drain on some kitchen paper and chop up. Add the fresh red pepper, if that is what you are using, to the frying pan with the tomatoes and garlic. Sauté them together for about 5 minutes until they have softened, then let them cool off.

Chuck the lot into your food processor or blender along with all the other ingredients, including the New Mexico or Spanish *ñoras*, if using, and chilli peppers. Blend well, then turn out into a dish. Let the sauce just sit there for a couple of hours for the flavours to develop, then whisk slightly before you use it.

Pickled Lemons or Limes

Limones y Limas en Adobo

PHOTOGRAPH OPPOSITE PAGE 72

These are a North African favourite with chicken, lamb and fish, rather like pickled onions with cheese.

Makes one large jar

12 small lemons or limes (you could use some of each)
Plenty of salt
1.8 litres (3 pints) spiced vinegar – you can buy this ready-made

You need 1 large, airtight preserving jar. Make sure it is well washed and sterilised. Give the lemons and limes a good scrub. Cut the lemons or limes almost but not quite into quarters, so that they still hold together at the stem. Sprinkle the cut flesh with salt, then close them. Pack them into the jar, sprinkling each layer generously with salt. Cover and leave for 10 days, until the fruits are well softened.

Tip the lemons and/or limes from the jar and wipe off the salt. Do not rinse with water, just wipe with kitchen paper. Heat the spiced vinegar until it is boiling, then pour over the fruit in a clean, sterilised jar. Store in a cool place for at least 4 weeks before using.

Fish Stock – A Spanish Way

Makes about 1 litre (1¾ pints)

900g (2lb) fish bits and pieces, including bones and heads
1 onion, quartered
1 carrot, peeled and quartered
1 stick of celery, roughly chopped
1 leek, sliced
150ml (¼ pint) dry white wine
1 litre (1¾ pints) cold water
A small bundle of fresh herbs –
for example, thyme, parsley and a bay leaf
Few white peppercorns

Whack all the ingredients into a very large pan, bring to the boil, cover and simmer for at least half an hour.

If you want a richer, more concentrated stock, reduce the liquid by bubbling it for longer. Strain through muslin or a fine sieve and discard everything apart from the stock itself. Skim and store in the refrigerator for up to 24 hours or freeze for up to 1 month.

Chicken Stock – A Spanish Way

Spanish stocks, whether meat, chicken, fish or game, don't really vary much from the stocks of the good cooks of France, England or Italy. This particular recipe was given to me by José Luis Izuel, a passionate amateur cook whose day job is as a picture restorer. He sometimes adds a ham bone too for flavour, a traditionally Spanish touch.

Makes about 900ml (1½ pints)

1 chicken carcass, plus any bones left over from carving the bird
1 onion, quartered
1 turnip, peeled and roughly chopped
1 small carrot
A small bundle of fresh herbs – for example, rosemary, thyme, parsley and a bay leaf
Few white peppercorns
½ teaspoon salt

Put the chicken carcass with any bones into a very large pan. Pour over about 1 litre (1¾ pints) cold water and bring this to the boil. Pop in the vegetables, herbs and peppercorns and simmer over a low heat with the lid on for at least 2 hours. Cool slightly, then strain through muslin or a fine sieve. Add salt to season.

Cool, and refrigerate when completely cold. Skim off any surface fat before you use the stock. You must use it within 2 days, or if you have frozen the stock, 3 months.

Game Stock

Follow the recipe for chicken stock, using the carcasses of game birds or the leftover meat of any game such as pheasant, pigeon, etc., to make a rich game stock.

Beef Stock – A Spanish Way

Makes about 1.5 litres (2½ pints)

Ask your butcher for some beef bones – I'm sure he'll oblige

450g (1lb) marrow bones
450g (1lb) shin of beef, cut into chunks
1 carrot, roughly chopped
1 onion, quartered
1 turnip, roughly chopped
2 sticks of celery, sliced
Few black peppercorns
A small bundle of fresh herbs – for example, marjoram, parsley, thyme and a bay leaf
½ teaspoon salt

Put the beef bones and shin of beef into a roasting pan and pop them into a preheated hot oven, 220°C/425°F (gas mark 7), for about half an hour to get them nice and brown. This is important if you want to develop a really good stock. Transfer them to a large saucepan and cover with 2 litres (3½ pints) cold water.

Roast the vegetables in the same roasting dish for about 15 minutes until they are brown too, then tip them into the pan with the bones. Heat until boiling, then reduce the heat and simmer for 2–3 hours with the lid on, not forgetting to add the peppercorns, herbs and salt.

Skim off any scum or fat from the surface of the stock pot from time to time, then cool a little and strain through muslin or a fine sieve. Cool completely and refrigerate. Use within 2 days, or freeze and use within 3 months. Skim off any fat from the surface before using the stock.

Veal or Lamb Stock

Follow the recipe for beef stock, using veal or lamb bones instead, but do not brown the vegetables – just roast them for a few minutes before adding them to the veal or lamb bones and water.

Soups and Tapas

Almond Cream Soup

Ajo Blanco

Barcelona, the city of Gaudí, Dali, pimps, whores, drug pushers, itinerant tango dancers, fabulous restaurants, brilliant bars – in short, the whole shebang of a culturally erotic city – is a superb place. It is a city like Avignon or Hamburg, a city of high art and low life, a city of style and a city of menace.

But if you find yourself spending twelve hours in Barcelona Airport, hustled and jostled by the great unwashed on their holidays, sitting on a comfortable seat if you can find one, with disinformation and misinformation about your departure time being the name of the game, then you would be extremely glad to leave it and get in a big silver bird that flies you away to Majorca.

And it was there we found ourselves at midnight – Pritchard, another bloke and me – screeching to a halt in our red open-topped Fiesta by the steps of the imposing Valparaiso Hotel, high above Palma harbour. Ancient and rustic flunkies opened doors, pushed and dragged bags while our heels clacked and clicked across the vast marble-floored foyer as we strode manfully several miles towards the reception desk.

Formalities over, signatures given, passports taken away, we walked another two or three miles to the bar and, like a jack-in-a-box, a sleepy bartender, white-coated with gold epaulettes, sprang to serve us in 0.5 of a second. We ordered some big ones. In the far, far distance a piano tinkled. It was the height of the summer season in Majorca, Juan Carlos was expected at any moment, Robert Maxwell's yacht was in the harbour, the boulevards were thronging, the weather was fine. And yet this massive, prestigious hotel was, except for Pritchard, the other chap and me, empty. Was this place a front for something else, something like – well, local orange laundering? What did the staff do when we three were the only guests? How could it keep going with nobody in it, we wondered. Of course, they assured us it was just a freak situation and normally it was terribly busy. We discovered that all the staff had been there more than twenty years and that the General Manager, one Enrique Anton Ortiz de Urbina, a multilingual, aristocratic fellow, was a superb host.

Anyway, to get back to this introduction to Almond Cream Soup, almonds grow in profusion in Majorca, no doubt a legacy of the Moors or indeed the Christians or was it the Jews or even the Phoenicians, because they certainly all came over on some pretext or other and left their culinary footprints on the island.

So Enrique said, 'Our chef is dead good at making Almond Cream Soup, which is a local speciality.' (That's the thing about all high-born Spanish, they speak English with American accents.) In the blazing noonday heat the next day, for some extraordinary reason, we found ourselves on the roof of the Valparaiso – me petrified of falling off the bloody roof and the tar sticking to my feet – while their head chef, in crisply-starched whites, made this wondrous little dish. He had peeled and ground the fresh almonds himself, which made this very delicate cream soup particularly good. And although it doesn't taste of cheese, it reminded me of that other wonderful soup, Stilton Soup. Do make sure that your ground almonds are as fresh as possible and haven't been sitting on the shelves of your local health food shop for the last six months.

Now for the recipe:

Almond Cream Soup

Serves 4–6

50g (2oz) butter
50g (2oz) plain flour
900ml (1½ pints) chicken stock –
use home-made if you possibly can
450ml (¾ pint) milk
100g (4oz) ground almonds
150ml (¼ pint) single cream
1 egg yolk
Salt
Ground white pepper (this avoids black specks in your soup)
A few extra ground almonds, for serving

Melt the butter in a large pan and blend in the flour to make a *roux*. Gradually whisk in the chicken stock and the milk to make a smooth, lump-free consistency. Heat until it is almost boiling, when the mixture will thicken to make the basis of this delicious cream soup. Turn down the heat to really low and simmer very gently for 15 minutes.

Scatter in the ground almonds and stir through, then cook for another 5 minutes. Now at this stage my friends at the Valparaiso Hotel strained the mixture through a sieve to give a super-smooth consistency, and you can do likewise if you wish, but it is not essential.

Just before serving, whisk together the cream and egg yolk and stir through the soup. Heat gently for a moment, but do not boil otherwise it will curdle. Season to taste and sprinkle a few ground almonds on the top of the soup.

Chilled Garlic and Almond Soup with Grapes

Sopa fría de Ajo y Almendras con Uvas

CENTRE-SPREAD PHOTOGRAPH BETWEEN PAGES 168 AND 169

We had been filming in a very beautiful fourteenth-century farmhouse up in the hills behind Calpe on the Costa Blanca with a mad, splendidly eccentric English winegrower called Peter Pateman. And to celebrate the event he had invited his chums round for a massive feast of roast suckling pig, a dish I normally adore. But it was near the end of the trip, my poor old liver had taken a bashing and I wasn't really in the mood for such rich food. Besides, it was a hot day and you know how it is when you have been cooking, cooking, cooking – your own appetite diminishes dramatically.

Sympathetic to my predicament, Peter's wife told me of a wonderful creamy iced soup made from almonds. Since they grew almonds on their farm she just happened to have all the appropriate ingredients. So, under her supervision, I made it. It has the most refreshing flavour, not dissimilar in some ways to an iced coconut soup I once had in Malaysia. It is a sort of white *gazpacho*.

I prepared the soup by hand and I have to admit it was a tiny bit lumpy – but the house didn't have electricity. It would be definitely brilliant if you could use a food processor or blender to give the same consistency as the iced yoghurt drink, *lassi*. And by the way, to continue the theme, if you added some chopped coriander into it as well, I reckon it would be ace.

Serves 8

4 slices of stale bread, crusts removed
4 cloves of garlic, peeled and very finely chopped
about 1.2 litres (2 pints) chilled water
225g (8oz) ground almonds
5 tablespoons olive oil
3 tablespoons good quality white wine vinegar
Salt
Sweet Muscat or Thompson grapes for garnish, seedless if possible
Squeeze of lemon juice, to prevent the grapes turning brown

Soak the stale bread in some water to soften it for 10 minutes or thereabouts, then squeeze out the water and put the bread into your food processor, along with the garlic and a splash of the chilled water. Blend it for a moment, then add the almonds and blend for a moment more. Keeping your processor on low, drizzle in the oil, then the vinegar, followed by the salt and lastly the rest of the water. Taste it, check the seasoning and add a touch more vinegar or salt if it is needed. The consistency should be fairly thick, but smooth. Tip into a big serving bowl and put in the fridge to chill through.

Next, put your feet up while you peel the grapes (believe me, it's therapeutic!). Take out the seeds if they have any and sprinkle them with a little lemon juice to keep their colour.

Whisk the soup before serving and garnish with grapes.

Gazpacho

The beach at Torremolinos is empty. The colourful beach bars are shuttered and the white apartment blocks are still. The Mediterranean laps gently in this warm early Spanish morning as a huge yellow sun eases itself over the far horizon. The crew are setting up their equipment. I am sitting on the gunnel of a large rowing boat, waiting for the fishermen to come. A yellow pie-dog, a breed thrown back to the time of the Pharaohs, is watching too, hoping for some food. He looks sinister and his short fur is stretched tight over his protruding ribs.

Everyone is subdued this morning. Last night we all drank too much in an appalling flamenco bar in Málaga, where fat overmade-up women in their garish 'traditional' costumes stomped round one thin, black-moustached, aquiline-nosed, weasel-faced man – the sort of guy who would have played an informer in one of those black and white B-movies about the German occupation of France in the Second World War. He would, of course, end up being shot.

The tranquillity of the morning is shattered by the arrival of Miguel, an ebullient little chap in neatly-pressed white trousers, deck shoes, blue-and-white-hooped top, and an admiral's cap with a pair of crossed anchors perched jauntily on his head. And two older, noisy, bow-legged men with deep guttural voices, who are the fishermen.

We push the boat into the sea and with slow, powerful, rhythmic strokes we row out, in a semicircle, feeding the net out behind us as we go. One end of the net is fastened to the shore. In twenty minutes the fishermen have completed the whole arc and we are back on shore. They are fishing in a way unchanged since biblical times. Four of us in line haul in the net, haul and gather, haul and gather. Towards the end the net becomes heavier and heavier. What will it reveal? It could be overflowing with shiny sardines or anchovies or maybe even with some plump bass or fluttering, tiny fish that the Spanish call *bocorones*.

I am doing my piece to camera as we strain on the net; it is really quite a moving experience. There is still no one stirring on the Strip behind us. Finally, the net is on the beach. Excitedly, we peer down and open it to reveal thirteen tiny, pathetic little fishes.

The Plan is, or rather the Plan was, to follow up this pastiche of traditional Spanish life with a cooking sketch. And I know He did a pretty good job with just five, but there ain't much I can do with this lot. We decide to go for Plan B. Plan B centres on Miguel's idea that strong, silent men who have been going about their business in small boats at sea, spending hours toiling, should walk 50 yards to their beach bar, open it up and have a few shots of brandy while deciding what to do next.

The sun is higher now. The thick black coffee laced with *Ciento y Tres* is terrific. Holiday-makers in track suits are beginning to appear. The waiters, white shirted and black waistcoated, open up the beach bars. Beach boys are laying out the deck chairs and the sun loungers, men in little bars are peeling potatoes, preparing Spanish omelettes, chopping up peppers and filleting anchovies to pickle in olive oil. Crates are being stacked, shelves filled, baskets of olives and tomatoes are being delivered and the air is filled with the aroma of olive oil. A boy is cleaning the beach, picking up cigarette ends and other debris.

Torremolinos, the Strip, is about to burst into another day of food, fun, sun and an awful lot of drink. And it was in the midst of this total, enjoyable, innocent, ingenuous situation that I suddenly decided to make the mother and father of all *gazpachos* in a large bucket, using a hand-held blender the size of a small outboard motor. And the secret flavour of the soup was that all the vegetables had been ripened in the hot Spanish sun. They were, as Miguel said, 'happy vegetables'.

Now for the recipe:

Gazpacho

Serves 12

1.5kg (3¼lb) fresh ripe tomatoes, skinned and roughly chopped (choose ones that have a really good flavour)
2 medium green peppers, cored, seeded and chopped into chunks
2 small onions, chopped
2 cucumbers, peeled and chopped
8 tablespoons red wine or sherry vinegar
1 teaspoon chopped fresh tarragon or ½ teaspoon dried
½ teaspoon sugar
2 cloves of garlic, chopped
250ml (8fl oz) tomato juice
250ml (8fl oz) iced water
Salt
Ice cubes

For the croûtons

100g (4oz) butter
2 slices of white bread, crusts removed, cut into small cubes
2 cloves of garlic, crushed (optional)

For the side dishes

Cucumber, green pepper, tomatoes, onions, all very finely chopped

Chuck all the ingredients except the garnishes into a food processor (in several batches) and blend well. It is rather like liquidising a salad. Check the seasoning before chilling it very well.

For the croûtons, melt the butter in a heavy frying pan. Add the bread cubes and cook gently, stirring and turning well, until they are golden and crunchy. Drain them on some kitchen paper and let them cool down. If you are a garlic fanatic, add the cloves of crushed garlic to the pan when you are frying the bread.

When you are serving the soup, pass round the garnishes and croûtons in separate little bowls.

Galician Stew

Cocido Gallego

CENTRE-SPREAD PHOTOGRAPH BETWEEN PAGES 168 AND 169

Virtually every garden, smallholding or farm in Galicia has a granary built of granite in which corn and potatoes can be stored for the winter. These curious little buildings, like emperors' tombs on stilts, are protected from the forces of evil by a Christian cross at one end and a pagan Celtic phallic-like symbol at the other.

Well, what has all this to do with the price of fish, I hear you cry? Nothing, really, except it is intriguing that there is a Celtic gastronomic theme, too, that threads its way from Galway to Cornwall, from Cornwall to Brittany, from Brittany to Galicia. Take the great Irish stew of boiled beef or bacon and cabbage and compare it with the Breton *kig ha farz* stew; take the original Cornish pasty and compare it with the Galician *empanada* (see page 123).

And here is another one that fits into this gastronomic jigsaw puzzle: the mighty *Cocido Gallego*, a really robust country stew. Not what you would do for an intimate dinner party *à deux*, but the sort of dish that would be terrific for a bonfire night party. Perversely, I cooked it in high summer in a vineyard next to one of those granaries I have been wittering on about. Although it took hours to prepare, there was no real effort involved, just time. It was truly a feast fit for farmers, prophets, poets and politicians, rampaging Vikings or mystical Celts.

Serves lots

175g (6oz) chick peas, soaked for a day in cold water
3.5–4.5kg (8–10lb) traditionally-cured ham joint, presoaked as above
1 beef or marrow bone, for enriching the flavour of the stock
225g (8oz) shin of beef, cut into large chunks
½ large 1.5kg (3½lb) free-range, corn-fed chicken
900g (2lb) potatoes, peeled and quartered
4–6 chorizo, *sliced*
1 large green Savoy cabbage, shredded
Freshly ground black pepper

Drain the soaking water from the chick peas and ham joint and rinse the ham in some fresh water. Put them into a huge cooking pot that has a lid with the beef or marrow bone and cover with cold water. Bring to the boil and skim the surface. Turn the heat to really low, put on the lid and cook for about 2 hours.

Come back to the kitchen and add the chopped beef to the pot. Go away again. Come back in half an hour to add the chicken and give this another half an hour. Skim any scum off the surface.

Now throw in the potatoes and cook gently for 30 minutes, then add the sliced *chorizo* and cabbage. Cook for another 20 minutes, or thereabouts. Fish out the ham and chicken and slice them, discarding all bones. Return the meats to the soup, taste and season with some black pepper. You won't need salt – enough will be provided by the ham.

You can eat the stock as a soup for the first course if you like, with the ham, sausage, chick peas and vegetables to follow – or just bung it into big bowls and eat it with large amounts of bread and wine.

Fifteen-Minute Soup

Sopa de un Cuarto de Hora

Serves 6

4 tablespoons olive oil
1 small onion, chopped
1 clove of garlic, crushed
50g (2oz) serrano *ham, cubed*
2 slices of stale white bread, crusts removed, then cubed
1 large tomato, skinned and chopped
450ml (3/4 pint) fish stock
450ml (3/4 pint) cold water
1/2 teaspoon crushed saffron strands
150ml (1/4 pint) dry sherry
1 dozen mussels or clams, well scrubbed (throw out any damaged ones or ones that do not shut when tapped)
1 dozen prawns, peeled
Salt
Freshly ground black pepper
2 tablespoons chopped fresh parsley, to garnish
1 egg, hard-boiled, shelled and chopped, to garnish

Heat the oil in a large saucepan and sauté the onion for about 3 minutes until softened, then add the garlic and fry for another minute. Throw in the ham, followed by the bread and tomato, stirring well. Tip in the stock and water, then add the saffron and sherry. Cook quite rapidly for 10 minutes, then lower the heat and chuck in the mussels or clams and prawns. Bubble gently for 5 more minutes, until the mussels – or clams – open (throw out any that don't). Taste and season the soup, then serve it, garnished with the parsley and egg. Enjoy it with some fresh crusty bread.

Salted Almonds

Almendras Saladas

The cheerful ritual of having little snacks washed down with wine or sherry every day before meals is an inseparable part of the Spanish way of life. Unless you count the English predilection for tea drinking there is nothing to compare with this passionate happy hour that takes place in bars the length and breadth of Spain at lunchtime and in the evening.

Tapa means cover and, according to my chum Miguel, in former times bar owners would give their customers a slice of bread to cover their wine between sips to keep flies and other insects out. Naturally, the drinkers began to nibble the bread as the evening wore on and so the tradition was born. Or not as the case may be.

Makes about 8 servings

225g (8oz) blanched almonds
5–6 tablespoons olive oil
(or about 100g [4oz] clarified butter, if you prefer)
Salt

If you have had to blanch the almonds yourself by plunging them into boiling water and peeling off the skins, you'll have to make sure you dry them well. Save yourself the trouble by buying them already blanched, but obviously fresh ones will be far and away better.

Heat the oil or clarified butter in a small heavy-based saucepan and gently fry about two dozen almonds at a time until they are a beautiful golden brown. Do take care that you don't burn them. Remove from the pan with a slotted spoon and pop them on to some kitchen paper to soak up any excess oil.

Now, while the nuts are still warm, sprinkle a large piece of greaseproof paper with the salt. Tip on the nuts and turn them, until they have a nice, lightly-salted coating. When they are quite cold, you can pop them into a screw-topped jar for storage – but I suspect they won't get that far as they taste so good.

PS To make devilled almonds, add a few grains of cayenne pepper to the salt before tipping on the nuts.

Spanish Croquettes

Croquettes are universally liked in Spain. Basically, you need a thick béchamel-flavoured sauce and filling of fish (shrimps, tuna or crab) or chicken, sweetcorn or mixed meat or whatever rolled in flour, dipped in eggwash and breadcrumbs and then deep-fried. You can make them any size or shape you like, from round to square, from tubes to ovals to little cylinders. They make wonderful *tapas*.

Be sure to deep-fat fry them and, as long as you have kept the mixture in the refrigerator beforehand, there is no danger of their disintegrating when they hit the hot fat.

Serves 12 for *tapas*

For the basic mix

5 tablespoons olive oil – or you could use 100g (4oz) butter

75g (3oz) plain flour

450ml (3/4 pint) liquid – use an equal amount of milk and chicken or fish stock, appropriate to your chosen filling

For the filling

175g (6oz) chopped cooked chicken, plus 1 teaspoon chopped fresh tarragon

or

175g (6oz) chopped peeled prawns or shrimps, plus 1/2 teaspoon paprika

or

175g (6oz) finely chopped serrano *ham, plus 1 teaspoon fresh chopped parsley*

For the coating

4 tablespoons plain flour

2 eggs

2 tablespoons milk

5 tablespoons white or brown fresh breadcrumbs

Salt

Freshly ground black pepper

To make the filling mix, heat the oil or melt the butter in a saucepan, then stir in the flour – it should froth a bit, but you don't want it to fry! Cook very gently for a minute, then gradually stir in the liquid, bringing it up to the boil so it thickens. Cook for a couple of minutes, then add your chosen flavourings. Pour the sauce into a shallow dish where it can cool and go firm. Leave for at least 3 hours – overnight is even better.

Next, you have to roll the mixture into balls or sausages – about 2 dozen in total. Put the coating ingredients out in three shallow bowls arranged in a line – first the flour, then the eggs beaten with the milk and lastly the breadcrumbs, seasoned with a little salt and pepper.

Dip the rolls into the coatings in the same sequence, then chill for at least half an hour. Fry in hot oil – about 2.5cm (1 inch) deep – until they are golden brown. Don't be tempted to try and cook too many at once. Drain on kitchen paper and eat shortly afterwards.

Pimiento and Anchovy Spread

Pasta de Untar de Pimientos y Anchoas

Makes about 24 *tapas*

4 canned pimientos, drained and finely chopped
100g (4oz) canned anchovy fillets, drained and chopped
1 small onion, very finely chopped
2 tablespoons fresh chopped parsley
2 tablespoons olive oil
3 teaspoons red wine vinegar
Freshly ground black pepper
6 slices of white or brown bread

This wonderful paste couldn't be simpler to make – just throw the lot into a bowl and squish it all together. Or you could pop everything into a blender and whizz it for a few moments. Either way, it improves with a little ageing, so keep it overnight in the fridge.

A day later, spread it on to the sliced bread and cut into shapes – squares, fingers, triangles, rhomboids, whatever.

PS While it is in the fridge, be sure to keep it covered as it is quite a fishy mix.

Potted Game

Guisado Cazadora

Makes enough for 6–8 as a starter

50g (2oz) streaky bacon, rind removed and finely chopped
225g (8oz) pig's liver, trimmed and sliced very thinly
1 wineglass fino *sherry*
Cold water
½ teaspoon paprika
½ teaspoon ground cinnamon
½ teaspoon ground cloves
Salt
Freshly ground black pepper
1 tablespoon ground almonds
450g (1lb) cooked game – use anything you like, for example, hare, partridge, venison or pheasant

Pop the streaky bacon into a frying pan and fry gently so that the fat runs. Add the pig's liver and cook quickly – about 1 minute on each side. Pour in the sherry and enough water to cover. Add the spices and some salt and pepper. Simmer gently for about 20 minutes, until the liver is tender. Allow to cool.

Tip the liver and bacon (reserving the cooking liquid) into a food processor or blender, adding the ground almonds and game. Blend for about 15–20 seconds or so, until a smooth paste is formed. It should have a thick but soft consistency – you may need to add 2–3 spoonfuls of the cooking liquid from the liver and bacon to get it just right. Season, pot and cool – then refrigerate. Spread it thickly on crusty bread or toast and use within 3–4 days.

Stuffed Eggs

Huevos Rellenos

Makes 24 *tapas*, 12 servings

1 dozen eggs
150ml (1/4 pint) mayonnaise – home-made is best
(see page 11)
12 green olives, chopped
1 × 200g (7oz) can pimientos, well drained
2 teaspoons lemon juice
Salt
Freshly ground black pepper

Hard-boil the eggs, first of all. Don't forget to plunge them into cold water when they're cooked – this prevents that nasty blackening around the yolk, as I'm sure you know. When they have cooled down, shell them and cut in half, lengthways. Remove the yolks.

Put half the egg yolks into a bowl and mash them down. Pour in the mayonnaise and mix well, then add most of the chopped olives. Reserve a few fine strips of pimiento for decoration and chop the rest. Mix these bits of pimiento into the mayonnaise and give it a good stir, adding the lemon juice and some salt and black pepper to season.

Next, you have to fill the empty egg whites with this mixture. You can pipe it in, but you may find that some of the bits bung up the nozzle, so I'd opt for a teaspoon.

Garnish these stuffed eggs with sieved egg yolk, little strips of pimiento and small pieces of olives.

Marinated Fish

Escabeche de Pescado

Serves lots

1.5kg (3½lb) fish – mackerel, herring, sardine, etc., filleted and sliced
75g (3oz) plain flour
7 tablespoons olive oil
5 cloves of garlic, crushed
3 bay leaves
1 teaspoon fresh oregano
1 teaspoon fresh thyme
3 whole cloves
12 peppercorns
3 teaspoons paprika
300ml (½ pint) white wine vinegar
300ml (½ pint) cold water
300ml (½ pint) dry white wine
2 teaspoons salt
1 dried red chilli pepper
Sliced raw onion, green or red pepper and tomato, to garnish

Lightly flour the pieces of fish and fry them in 2–3 tablespoons of the oil for about 3 to 5 minutes, depending on their thickness, removing each piece as it is cooked. Allow them to cool, then place in a shallow earthenware container or other suitable serving dish.

Add the remaining oil to the frying pan and heat it, then add the garlic, together with all the other herbs and spices, except the paprika. Stir them around briefly, then remove the pan from the heat. Now stir in the paprika.

In a large saucepan, bring the vinegar, water and wine up to boiling point. Lower the heat and add the oil and seasoning mixture. Cook together for a minute or two then remove from the heat and allow to cool down for 10 minutes or so. Stir in the salt and chilli pepper.

Next, pour this mixture over the fish fillets and leave them to marinate, covered, for at least 24 hours. Keep refrigerated but allow time for it to come to room temperature before serving – this way you can really taste all the superb flavours.

Before you dish up, scatter some thinly-sliced onion, pepper and/or tomato over the fish to garnish it.

Fried Squid

Calamares Fritos

Serves 4 as a starter or *tapas*

450g (1lb) squid, prepared by you or your fishmonger and cut into rings or tentacle lengths
6 tablespoons plain flour
2 eggs, beaten
Oil for shallow or deep frying
Salt
Lemon wedges, for garnishing

Rinse the prepared squid well, then pop it on to some kitchen paper to dry. Put the flour into a shallow bowl and coat the squid pieces in it, then dip them in beaten egg.

Heat up the oil – you need it to a depth of at least 12mm (½ inch) if you're shallow frying. When it's hot (test by dropping in a cube of bread to see if it sizzles), pop in the squid, a few bits at a time, and fry until they are a light golden brown. Avoid overcooking them – they will need a couple of minutes only. You may find that they will spit rather alarmingly at you, so a pan lid is good protection.

Drain them well on kitchen paper and serve sprinkled with a little salt and garnished with the lemon wedges. They taste pretty good with mayonnaise (see page 11).

Snails

Caracoles

It should not be assumed that just because we film a restaurant we are endorsing the quality of its food. Sometimes we choose it simply because of its decor or ambience, which is suitable for our purposes.

The restaurant called Los Caracoles in Barcelona was, however, an exception. It did have a spectacular appearance – outside the entrance the roaring, ancient spit turning spluttering, golden, fat chickens over a wood brazier and inside the highly decorated wine barrels, rumbustious Renaissance oil paintings, fine tiles and Spanish oak make it the most dazzling place. Best of all, though, is the kitchen. It has a huge, black, rumbling coal-fire range probably 18 feet long by 6 or 7 wide, around which cider-swigging, sweating chefs toil ceaselessly, producing roast suckling pig, whole legs of lamb, mountains of hake and potatoes amid much shouting, yelling, excitement and tension. Piles of *gambas* (prawns) are sizzled on griddles. Heavy black trays, groaning with baked tomatoes, peppers and onions, are crashed in and out of ovens. For those of you who have read Mervyn Peake's brilliant *Gormenghast* trilogy, you will remember the black Gothic kitchen so vividly described therein, presided over by the tyrant chef, Swelter. And I reckon this is Swelter's kitchen.

Los Caracoles means snails as you probably know, and this place serves thousands of portions of them a week from huge cauldrons. And if you have only ever eaten half-a-dozen snails from a neat Le Creuset dish with garlic butter you have a delightful treat in store if you can make your way to this place and consume a plate or two of these delicious things. But failing that, here is a recipe to make at home.

Serves 4

6–12 snails per person, depending on their size
(the snail, not the person)

For the sauce

3 tablespoons olive oil
2–3 pork ribs, chopped
Cured ham bone and knuckle
1 onion, finely sliced
4 cloves of garlic, finely chopped
1 bay leaf
1 sprig of thyme
450g (1lb) tomatoes, skinned and chopped
600ml (1 pint) red wine
600ml (1 pint) chicken stock
2 tablespoons chopped fresh parsley, to garnish

The best way to clean the snails is to starve them in a ventilated box or a covered pail for a week, giving them a shower of fresh water every now and again. (You have to think ahead for this recipe!) Or you could buy canned or frozen ones, which are already blanched.

To cook the snails, put them in a pan of cool water and bring them slowly to the boil. This way you will be able to extract them from their shells quite easily later. Cook the snails for about 1 hour, simmering gently. Take off the heat when they're done, rinse and strain.

For the sauce, heat the oil in a large pan. Put the pork ribs with the ham bone and knuckle into the pot and sauté these for 10 minutes. Add the onion and garlic and stir well, sautéeing gently for about 20 minutes, until the onion is really soft.

Pop the bay leaf and thyme into the pan, then add the tomatoes, stirring them together while they fry for 10 minutes.

Pour in the wine and stock and cook for 30–40 minutes. You can cook them for longer if you want to reduce and concentrate the flavours further. Don't put on the lid because you want the sauce to reduce, but keep an eye on the level of the liquid and top up if you need to. Remove the bay leaf.

The sauce is best left for a few hours before serving – overnight is even better – so that the flavours develop. Then reheat the snails and sauce together and garnish with the chopped parsley.

Spiced Pigeon

Pichón Sazonado con Especias

For 16 *tapas*

8 tablespoons olive oil
4 pigeons, cleaned and quartered
2 bulbs of garlic, separated into cloves, but not peeled
2 onions, chopped
1 tablespoon wine vinegar
250ml (8fl oz) fino *sherry*
2 bay leaves
Salt
Freshly ground black pepper

Heat the oil in a large frying pan and pop in the pigeons. Fry them for a couple of minutes, turning over frequently to brown them, then add the garlic cloves and chopped onions. Sauté for a minute, then pour in the wine vinegar and sherry, not forgetting to add the bay leaves and seasonings.

Bring the lot to the boil, lower the heat and simmer, covered, for about 30 minutes. Remove the lid and bubble gently for 10 minutes more, so that the liquid reduces slightly. By now the birds should be tender – prod them with a fork to find out. If they seem tough, cook a little longer. Fish out and discard the bay leaves. Serve as a drinks snack with iced *fino* or *manzanilla* sherry.

Fish and Shellfish

Sardines with Oregano

Sardinas con Orégano

Serves 4

450g (1lb) fresh sardines, cleaned and washed
150ml (1/4 pint) olive oil
2 cloves of garlic, crushed
4 tablespoons chopped fresh oregano
175ml (6fl oz) white wine vinegar
175ml (6fl oz) cold water
Salt
Freshly ground black pepper

Fry the sardines in the oil, which you've heated up in a large frying pan. Cook for about 2–3 minutes on each side. Transfer to a large flameproof casserole and tip a little of the oil from the pan over them.

Mix together the garlic, oregano, vinegar and water. Season this with some salt and pepper and pour over the sardines. Bring to the boil slowly, then reduce the heat and simmer for 5 minutes. Let the fish cool down before you eat them.

Baked Basque Fish

Pescado asado a la Vasca

The Basque people certainly know how to make the best of fish. Fresh cod holds its own in Basque cooking – here's a good example.

Serves 4

You will need four pieces of foil, 30cm (12 inches) square
4 × 175g (6oz) white fish fillets, skinned – cod or haddock
50g (2oz) butter
1 small green pepper, cored, seeded and chopped
1 medium onion, finely chopped
1 clove of garlic, crushed
1 large tomato, skinned, seeded and chopped
2 bay leaves
8 tablespoons dry white wine
Juice of 1/2 lemon
Salt
Freshly ground black pepper

Position a piece of fish on each buttered foil square. Mix together all the vegetables and divide them up equally to cover the fish. Top each little pile of vegetables with half a bay leaf and 2 tablespoons wine, followed by a good squeeze of lemon juice. Season well, then fold the edges of the foil together to make four slightly baggy parcels.

Pop these parcels on to a baking sheet and cook them in a preheated oven, 190°C/375°F (gas mark 5), for about 30 minutes. However, it is not a bad idea to check one parcel after 20 minutes, as overcooking fish is a punishable offence. The fish is cooked when its flesh is opaque and flakes easily; the vegetables are cooked when they're tender. Serve with some lovely buttery new potatoes.

Opposite: ***Above*** Mountain Breakfast (page 174); ***Below*** Migas (page 172)
Next page, from left to right: Salt Cod with Chick Peas (page 56); Salt Cod and Orange Salad (page 55); Baked Bream, Madrid-Style (page 41)

Baked Bream, Madrid-Style

Dorada asada a la Madrileña

CENTRE-SPREAD PHOTOGRAPH BETWEEN PAGES 40 AND 41

Serves 4

1 whole bream, weighing about 900g (2lb), cleaned and scaled – ask your fishmonger to do this for you
Salt
4 lemon wedges
3 tablespoons lemon juice
4 tablespoons chopped fresh parsley
3 tablespoons fresh white breadcrumbs
1 bay leaf, torn into pieces
3–4 cloves of garlic, finely chopped
3 tablespoons olive oil
250ml (8fl oz) dry white wine
Freshly ground black pepper
Chopped black olives, to garnish

Rub the bream both inside and out with some salt. Make four diagonal cuts in the skin on one side of the fish and push a lemon wedge into each slit. Pour over the lemon juice and leave for about 20 minutes, giving you plenty of time to preheat the oven to 180°C/350°F (gas mark 4) and to enjoy a glass of wine. Oh, and you could mix together the parsley, breadcrumbs, bay leaf bits and chopped garlic.

Find a flameproof dish the right size for the fish, and heat the oil in it – just pop it in the oven for a couple of minutes. Now lay the fish in it and sprinkle the parsley and breadcrumb mixture over the top. Pour the wine around the fish and bring it up to bubbling point on the top of the stove. Transfer to the oven and bake for roughly half an hour, until the fish has cooked through. Baste a couple of times while it is cooking, adding a splash more white wine if you need (or want) to.

Season to taste with black pepper and toss on some chopped olives. Serve with a dish of steamy-hot potatoes, a green salad and a dry white or light red wine.

Above Mussels and Clams in Tomato and Wine Sauce (page 70); ***Below left*** Hake with Potatoes and Garlic (page 46); ***Below right*** Fisherman's Hotpot (page 44)

Aromatic Sauté of Fresh Fish

Zarzuela

Every cookery book mentions without fail that the Spanish name of this dish, *zarzuela*, actually means 'a satirical light opera', though the connection between the music and the dish is, to say the least, tenuous. I once asked the humorist Miles Kington to write a rather different introduction to my *zarzuela* recipe and he produced a side-splittingly funny spoof about it being the signature dish of a well-known island slightly south of Gibraltar and north of Algiers. It was named after, he explained, the hollowed-out sea urchin used by the natives when cooking it.

By the way, *zarzuela* is a delightful fish stew and if you hold an empty sea urchin to your ear you might just hear the strains of the South Pacific.

Serves 6

150ml (1/4 pint) olive oil
12 king prawns, with the shells left on
1 medium onion, finely chopped
3 cloves of garlic, crushed
2 large tomatoes, skinned, seeded and chopped
1–2 tablespoons chopped fresh parsley
Salt
Freshly ground black pepper
2–3 tablespoons brandy (Spanish, of course)
1 bay leaf
1 teaspoon paprika
1 dried red chilli pepper, seeded and finely chopped
250ml (8fl oz) dry white wine
150ml (1/4 pint) fish stock
A few strands of saffron
6 × 175g (6oz) fish steaks – choose from two types, for example, hake, monkfish, cod, halibut
6 small squid, cleaned and cut into rings (see the notes on page 205)
12 mussels, well scrubbed (throw out any damaged ones)
Croûtons and chopped fresh chives, to garnish

Heat the oil in a very large frying pan and sauté the prawns. The moment they turn pink, remove them from the pan – you must avoid overcooking them. Pop them on one side.

In the same pan, fry together the onion and garlic for a minute or two, then throw in the tomatoes with the parsley and some salt and pepper. When the onion is soft, pour on the brandy and flame it. When the flames have subsided – hopefully without setting fire to your kitchen – you can proceed.

Add the bay leaf, paprika, chilli pepper, wine and fish stock, together with a few strands of saffron. Stir everything together well.

Next, you have to pop in the fish steaks and squid, adding a bit more seasoning. Bring up to the boil, then reduce the heat and simmer for about 8 minutes, shaking the pan from time to time to make sure that the fish doesn't stick. Pop in the mussels and cook with the lid on for about 10 minutes, until they open. (Make sure you throw out any that remain shut.) Put the prawns back in the pan and cook gently for a couple of minutes to heat through. Fish out and discard the bay leaf.

Transfer to a serving dish and strew the croûtons and chopped chives liberally over the top.

Fisherman's Hotpot

Puchero caliente estilo Pescador

PHOTOGRAPH OPPOSITE PAGE 41

Leaving the horseshoe bay of San Sebastián, we travelled to Guetaría along a coastal road similar to that between Teignmouth and Dawlish, for those of you who know Devon. Here, on a misty morning, we set out on yet another fishing trip (the director likes these) on a boat named after a Basque seabird, *Kulixka*. It was a delightful location for a cooking sketch.

Our skipper insisted that we try the traditional Basque fisherman's elevenses tipple, a white wine called Txacoli in Basque and Chacolí in Spanish, which is a little like cider, definitely an acquired taste, and is very cloudy. Not for me.

Anyway, I prepared this dish, watched a swimming race from Guetaría to Zarauz, three and a half miles away, and cheered on a brightly-painted whaler that was racing its rival from Zarauz while my traditional hotpot simmered away. It is a sort of fisherman's version of Irish stew, but with a Spanish flavour. It has boiled fish and potatoes, just like the boiled potatoes and pieces of lamb in an Irish stew.

Serves 4–6

4–6 × 175g (6oz) fish steaks – tuna, shark, cod, or whatever you like
Salt
4–6 tablespoons olive oil
2 large onions, sliced
900g (2lb) potatoes, thickly sliced
1.25kg (3lb) tomatoes, seeded and chopped
3 red or green peppers, cored, seeded and chopped
2 cloves of garlic, finely chopped
2 tablespoons chopped fresh parsley
2 bay leaves
Freshly ground black pepper

Rinse the fish steaks and pat them dry with some kitchen paper. Pop them on to a plate, season with salt and spoon over the oil. Just let them sit there for 10 minutes or so while you carry on.

Put the sliced onions and potatoes into a very large shallow pan with just enough boiling, salted water to cover. Add all the chopped tomatoes and stir them in well, then add the peppers and mix them in too. Put in the garlic and parsley with the bay leaves and add a little more salt and some freshly ground black pepper.

Sit the fish steaks on top of the other ingredients and simmer the pot gently without a lid for about 45 minutes, depending on the thickness of the steaks. If you are using fish other than tuna, you need to add it after 15 minutes' cooking time, and make sure you submerge it. Otherwise, make sure you baste the fish often to keep it moist.

You may need to remove the fish just before you're ready for dishing out, so that you can let the liquid in the pot bubble up and reduce for 3 or 4 minutes. Don't worry if the onions and potatoes have stuck to the pan at the bottom. They will brown nicely and taste delicious. Fish out the bay leaves before serving.

Any leftovers of this dish make a brilliant hash – *ropa vieja* as the Spanish call it, which literally translated means old clothes.

Hake with Potatoes and Garlic

Merluza con Patatas y Ajo

PHOTOGRAPH OPPOSITE PAGE 41

It was a hot day and after a long journey in a pathetic little car without air conditioning I was tired, thirsty and irritable, and not at all in the mood for monasteries. But as I rounded a bend on this tortuous road, the land dropped away to reveal a serene valley and an impressive granite monastery dating from the fifteenth century, set in neatly cultivated vegetable gardens.

But as we approached the front of the edifice I was astounded to see a massive coach park, souvenir shops, bars and throngs of people milling about smoking, drinking and eating, for all the world as if they were visiting Disneyland. You could buy holy honey, holy wine, holy candles, holy cassettes of the monks' greatest hits, Gregorian chants volumes 1 and 2, and all manner of holy artifacts.

I hadn't realised that monasteries are big business these days. And I felt, I must say, a little upset, a little cheated by this brash commercial approach to support what I had always assumed was the quiet, self-sacrificial, contemplative life. So, with thoughts of the old jingle 'I am but a poor wandering monk with only one dirty habit' racing through my mind, I swung jauntily on the massive bell-pull and waited to be admitted.

A long way off a bell rang and reverberated in some far-off cloister, and minutes passed before heavy bolts slipped back and the huge door opened to reveal a mild, gentle-looking monk who shook my hand and bade me come in.

My judgement had been hasty and incorrect. Within the monastery proper, quiet, genial and sincere men went about their work and their devotions with integrity and commitment. In fact, this place, the Cistercian Monastery of Osera, is I think where Graham Greene often retreated.

Normally, when we are away filming, we are a noisy, irreverent bunch, fond of telling rude jokes and using pretty bad language. But here we behaved perfectly, I am pleased to say, and felt spiritually cleansed by this brief encounter with people who had given up – or had never contemplated – jet-setting around the world slurping champagne and eating caviar, as is my unhappy lot.

Anyway, I cooked them some poached hake and promised to return one day, without cameras and the temporary glitz of a film crew.

Serves 4

1 onion, peeled and cut in half (for flavour only)
1 red pepper } cored, seeded and
1 green or yellow pepper } sliced lengthways
8 potatoes, peeled and sliced
4 × 175g (6oz) hake cutlets
6 tablespoons olive oil
4 cloves of garlic, crushed
2 tablespoons paprika (heaped)
Lemon wedges, to garnish

Bring two pans of salted water to the boil and add half an onion to each pot. Put the peppers into one pot and the potatoes into the other. Bring to the boil and simmer for 10 minutes. Now put the fish cutlets into the pot with the peppers and poach gently for 5 minutes – remember, always slightly undercook fish. Drain the fish, peppers and potatoes and keep warm.

To make the sauce, heat the oil in a frying pan and gently fry the garlic for a couple of minutes, making sure it doesn't burn. This forms the basis of the sauce. Take the pan off the heat, wait for a moment, then stir in the paprika, blending it in well. Let it settle, so that the paprika will flavour the oil.

Layer the cooked potatoes, peppers and poached hake on a warm serving dish and spoon the flavoured aromatic oil over the top. Serve, garnished with the lemon wedges, and eat at once.

Hake in Brandy

Merluza en Coñac

Hake, which is in the same family as haddock and cod, is probably Spain's most popular fish. And there are lots of them off the Mediterranean coast and in the Bay of Biscay. Or rather there used to be. But now, because of the global warming thing everyone is wittering on about, hake are migrating further north and, much to the consternation of British and Irish fishermen, the old hake have upsticked and taken residence in the Irish Sea, which has become warmer.

But to go back to the recipe. Fresh hake is marvellous and whether you just grill it and serve with some parsley sauce or even pan-fry a fillet with a little butter and lemon, you can't beat it. I invented this recipe in a moment of desperation on the harbour wall at Andraitx, to celebrate our happy sojourn in Majorca.

Serves 4

4 × 175g (6oz) hake cutlets
3 or 4 saffron strands, crushed
4 tablespoons olive oil
1 onion, finely chopped
2 cloves of garlic, finely chopped
4 tomatoes, skinned and chopped
1 tablespoon chopped fresh parsley
3–4 tablespoons Spanish brandy
24 mussels, well scrubbed (throw out any damaged ones or ones that remain closed when tapped)
1 wineglass dry white wine
Salt
Freshly ground black pepper

Rinse the hake cutlets and pat them dry with kitchen paper, then rub the crushed saffron over them.

Heat the oil in a large frying pan and fry together the onion and garlic for about 10 minutes until softened. Tip in the tomatoes and parsley and cook for at least 30 minutes, so the tomatoes and onions liaise into a thick, rich sauce. Then pop in the fish steaks. Turn up the heat to really get them going, turning them over after 1 minute.

Cook for a minute or so on the second side, then add the brandy and mussels, closely followed by the wine. Season with some salt and pepper and simmer gently for 15 minutes.

Serve, strewn with some more parsley, with a bowl of buttered new potatoes and a crisp salad.

Salmon with Clams

Salmón con Almejas

Spanish restaurants don't normally get going for dinner much before nine o'clock, often nearer ten. But on this day in my chum Moncho's restaurant, Casa Vilas in Santiago, there was unprecedented activity well before. The President of Galicia, Señor Fraga Iribarne, was coming to dinner and I was to cook for him.

The place was throbbing with security men, policemen, journalists, photographers, Press agents, public relations people, Tourist Board officials and film crews, including our own. Excitement was rather high. The President, a former Spanish ambassador to the Court of St James, is a powerful, important and respected man.

In anticipation of his arrival, we formed a sort of Guard of Honour. There would be much handshaking, bowing and scraping. Just a few minutes before the President was due to arrive I received, to put it politely, an urgent and unexpected call of nature. And clutching a handkerchief in front of my mouth and my hand to my stomach, I ran for the loo and locked myself in. But I was too late. And sparing you the gory details, suffice it to say I could not go out because my clothes were in no fit state to be seen in public, let alone on TV, and least of all in front of the President.

I tried to attract Pritchard's attention but he, of course, was busy shouting for me and didn't hear my plaintive cries for help. Finally, I did manage to catch his eye and explained my predicament.

'Oh, great!' he said and, at the top of his voice shouted out, 'For Christ's sake, get a new pair of trousers and a jacket for Floyd, he's had an accident in the lavatory.'

I felt not only ill but sorely humiliated.

Anyway, emerging wearing a chef's jacket size 48" (I take 42") and a pair of trousers built for a 6' 6" chef, I managed to greet the President and prepared him this simple little salmon dish.

Serves 4

4 × 175–225g (6–8oz) salmon fillets
50g (2oz) seasoned flour
4 tablespoons olive oil
1 large onion, finely chopped
2 cloves of garlic, crushed
675g (1½lb) clams in their shells, well scrubbed
300ml (½ pint) fish stock (make your own by boiling up some fish bits and bones with a bouquet garni – see page 16, or resort to a tub of the liquid stock you can now buy for speed)
1 wineglass dry white wine – Albarino works wonderfully
3 tablespoons lemon juice
A handful of fresh chopped parsley
1 teaspoon mustard paste
Salt
Freshly ground black pepper

Dust the salmon fillets in some seasoned flour and put them to one side while you create some glorious aromas by sautéeing together the onion and garlic in the oil (do this in a very large frying pan). When they have softened after 2 or 3 minutes, lay the salmon in the pan and cook the fillets for 2 minutes on each side.

Add the clams to the pan with the fish stock, wine, lemon juice and chopped parsley and cook for a little while. Five minutes should be ample time, as the salmon and clams must not overcook. This gives you the chance to throw a fresh, green salad together and slice up some crusty, wholemeal bread.

Just before serving, stir the mustard paste through the sauce and season with a little extra salt and pepper if you need to.

Hake with Clams, Asparagus and Peas

Merluza con Almejas, Espárragos y Guisantes

Serves 4

4 × 175g (6oz) hake cutlets
2 tablespoons plain flour
Salt
Freshly ground black pepper
3 tablespoons olive oil
2 medium onions, chopped
2 wineglasses dry white wine
1 wineglass cold water
A dozen or so clams, well scrubbed
(throw out any damaged ones)
50g (2oz) petit pois
2 eggs, hard-boiled and chopped
3 tablespoons chopped fresh parsley
225g (8oz) fresh, young, cooked asparagus spears
(the Spanish often use canned)

Rinse the fish and pat dry with kitchen paper, then roll in some flour, seasoned with salt and black pepper.

Heat the oil in a large frying pan that has a lid and sauté the chopped onions until they are well reduced. Add the hake cutlets to the pan and continue cooking gently for about 5 minutes, turning the fish over once. Add the wine and water, bring up to bubbling point and pop in the clams and peas.

Put on the lid and carry on cooking for about 5 minutes, until the clams open.

Check the fish from time to time as you don't want it to overcook. (The flesh should look opaque and should flake easily.) When it is ready, transfer to a warmed serving plate with the clams (discarding any which still haven't opened). Keep warm.

Add the chopped hard-boiled egg and most of the parsley to the liquid in the pan. Stir well and check the seasoning. It is unlikely that you will need any more salt. Be careful not to boil the sauce.

Arrange the cooked asparagus around the seafood and pour over the sauce. Serve straight away, sprinkled with the rest of the parsley.

Oven-baked Fish and Potato Pie

Pucherode Pescado

One of the few things that irritates me about the Spanish style of cooking is that in a dish like this one, which is effectively a Mediterranean Lancashire hotpot only made with fish, if you get my drift, they are sloppy about boning and skinning fish. My chum Carmen, who told me about this recipe, insisted that I use cutlets of fish complete with bone and skin. I think it would be vastly improved if you used thick fillets of any firm-fleshed white fish, such as cod, haddock, hake or monkfish – but completely free of bone and skin.

Serves 4

150ml (5fl oz) olive oil
900g (2lb) potatoes, sliced 7mm (1/4 inch) thick at the most
2 medium onions, sliced into fine rings
4 × 175g (6oz) firm-fleshed white fish fillets – hake is ideal
25g (1oz) plain flour
300ml (10fl oz) fresh tomato sauce – just liquidise some skinned ripe tomatoes for this dish
3 cloves of garlic, not chopped
1 tablespoon paprika
150ml (1/4 pint) fish stock
Salt
Freshly ground black pepper
3–4 handfuls of fresh white breadcrumbs
Dry white wine
Pernod

In a very large frying pan heat the oil and pop in the potatoes for about 30 seconds, turning them over once just so that they absorb some of the flavour. Remove them, and do the same with the onions. Remove these, then fry the fish fillets, which you have dredged with flour, in the oil for about half a minute on each side. Turn off the heat.

Now get a large casserole dish and put the potatoes into it, then layer the onions, fresh tomato sauce, garlic and paprika with the fish cutlets on top. Pour over the fish stock, season with salt and pepper and scatter over the breadcrumbs. Bake in a preheated oven, 190°C/375°F (gas mark 5), for 30–40 minutes.

Halfway through the cooking time, take the casserole out of the oven and splosh on some white wine and a dash of Pernod to moisten it – and a little more fish stock if it is needed. Serve with a green salad.

Grouper, Majorcan-Style

Grouper a la Mallorquina

Serves 6

6 tablespoons olive oil
900g (2lb) potatoes, peeled and sliced
4 × 175–200g (6–7oz) grouper fillets or steaks – you could use sea bass instead
2 tablespoons plain flour

For the sauce

4 tablespoons olive oil
1 medium onion, chopped
1 leek, trimmed and sliced
6 spring onions, finely sliced
1 red pepper, cored, seeded and chopped
2 handfuls of fresh Swiss chard or spinach, well washed, trimmed and sliced
2–3 cloves of garlic
1 tablespoon fresh chopped parsley
1 bay leaf
300ml (1/2 pint) fish stock
300ml (1/2 pint) fresh tomato sauce (see page 13)
1 tablespoon anis
25g (1oz) pine nuts
25g (1oz) sultanas
Salt
Freshly ground black pepper

First, make the sauce. Heat 4 tablespoons of oil in a saucepan and throw in all the vegetables and garlic, cooking briskly for about 5 minutes, stirring frequently. Add the parsley and bay leaf and pour in the fish stock and tomato sauce. Spoon in the anis liqueur. Simmer together everything for about 30 minutes or so, then add the pine nuts and sultanas. Season with some salt and pepper.

Heat 4 tablespoons of the oil in a large flameproof casserole and fry the potatoes gently for about 20 minutes, turning them over occasionally so they cook evenly.

Dust the fish fillets or steaks in the flour, then fry them briefly – about 2–3 minutes – in the rest of the oil. Remove from the pan and put to one side.

Return to the potatoes in the casserole, which should by now have cooked nicely. Arrange the fish on top of the potatoes and pour over the sauce. Pop on the lid and bake in a preheated oven, 180°C/350°F (gas mark 4), for about 15–20 minutes.

Serve with a glass or three of your favourite Spanish wine.

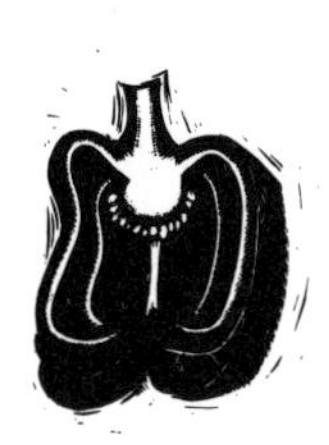

Salt Cod and Orange Salad

Bacalao con Ensalada de Naranja

CENTRE-SPREAD PHOTOGRAPH BETWEEN PAGES 40 AND 41

A brilliant salad – colourful and flavourful, with delicious contrasts between the saltiness of the cod and the sweetness of the oranges. Serve chilled.

Serves 4

450g (1lb) salt cod
5 tablespoons olive oil
6 oranges
1 large onion, finely chopped
100g (4oz) black or green olives
(rinse these well if they are in brine), halved
4 hard-boiled eggs – reserve a few slices for garnish and chop the rest
1 tablespoon white wine vinegar
Freshly ground black pepper

Most recipes using salt cod require you to soak the fish for a few hours first, but with this you slap it on to a hot griddle for about 2 minutes on each side to brown it. Remove any skin and bones from the fish, then tear it into shreds with your fingers. Put the shreds of cod into an earthenware dish and pour over the oil. Leave to marinate for at least 3 hours, overnight is even better.

When you are ready for assembly, peel the oranges, remove all the pith, divide into segments and then halve each segment. Place in a serving bowl with the drained cod (keep the oil), the onion, olives and chopped eggs. Mix well and dress with the reserved oil and the vinegar. Taste and adjust the seasoning, although it is unlikely that you will need more salt. Use the sliced egg for garnishing, if you like.

Salt Cod with Chick Peas

Bacalao con Garbanzos

CENTRE-SPREAD PHOTOGRAPH BETWEEN PAGES 40 AND 41

A kilometre outside Toledo, on top of a hill, there is a parador with an enormous terrace, from which there is a spectacular view of the city with its towers, battlements, churches and castles. It would have been a nice place to stay but unfortunately it was fully booked. However, they were kind enough to let me use their kitchen and there I prepared a dish using one of my favourite – and certainly one of the Spanish people's favourite – ingredients, salt cod.

Before refrigeration, salting was one of the main methods of preserving food and the tradition lives happily on because the thick, salted slabs of firm-fleshed milky-white cod make it unquestionably one of the greatest fish available. The salting makes it slightly tougher than fresh cod, but gives it a more meaty texture. After it has been soaked overnight in water and well rinsed to remove the salt, it has a unique flavour.

Incidentally, many bars offer as an excellent *tapa* a little cube of raw salt cod stuck with a toothpick to a fresh raw broad bean.

The dish that I quote below would centuries ago probably just have been cod and potatoes stewed together. But the Arab influence of chick peas and spinach makes it really interesting.

Serves 4–6

450g (1lb) chick peas, soaked for 24 hours
450g (1lb) salt cod, soaked for 24 hours and cut into pieces
225g (8oz) potatoes, peeled and cut into small chunks
6 tablespoons olive oil
2 cloves of garlic, chopped
1 thick slice of bread, crusts removed
Few strands of saffron
225g (8oz) fresh spinach, well washed and trimmed
Salt
Freshly ground black pepper

Drain the chick peas and salt cod, rinsing both in fresh water. Now put the chick peas into a large flameproof cooking pot with some cold water, bring to the boil, then simmer gently until they are almost cooked – they will need about 1½ hours, but add the salt cod and spuds after about 1 hour.

When they are nearly done, heat the oil in a frying pan and sauté the garlic and bread until both are golden brown. Drain them on some kitchen paper, then pound them down with the strands of saffron to make a glorious golden paste.

Cook the spinach briefly in a tiny amount of water, drain well and squeeze out the excess liquid. Chop it up a bit and fry in what is left of the oil, then add it to the chick peas and salt cod.

Go back to your golden paste and add a little hot water. Mix it through, then add to the pot with the chick peas and fish. Simmer everything together for 10 minutes or so, until the sauce thickens and is golden. Taste it and season. I am sure you will need some pepper but go easy on the salt.

Salt Cod in Garlic Sauce

Bacalao al Pil-Pil

After we had finished filming at Laguardia, a splendid walled town in the Rioja country, we drove to Bilbao from where we were to fly to Barcelona. I was pleased to be going back to Bilbao because years ago I had sailed there and had found a wonderful street full of *tapas* bars and little restaurants. We had spent a happy evening zig-zagging from one to the other, eating olives, ham, fish, salt cod, broad beans and all manner of wonderful things, washed down with lashings and lashings of wine. I am particularly fond of salt cod and in that street was a restaurant where I had had a wonderful dish of the stuff.

So I said to my assistant, Anne, 'Let's go to Bilbao early, then I can take you to this wonderful restaurant and research a few recipes at the same time [Ed., please note], have a brilliant meal and then catch the plane to Barcelona.' But after a couple of fruitless hours searching for the place I was damned if I could find it. Anne was becoming a bit po-faced and my enthusiasm was waning, so we decided to check ourselves in at the airport and take pot luck at the restaurant there.

Bilbao Airport is a tacky, untidy place – I think they are planning to rebuild it shortly. We looked at the self-service cafeteria; it was grim.

Mountains of cling-wrapped butterless sandwiches and a few sorry-looking dishes of *tapas*. So two discouraged and disgruntled pilgrims wandered into the restaurant, which was also purple, brown and gloomy.

But every cloud has a silver lining; there was salt cod on the menu, a dish known as *Bacalao al Pil-Pil*. This is a slab of cod sitting in what looks like a thin custard. Except the custard tastes of garlic and when you eat it you can tell at once that it is not a garlic-flavoured hollandaise sauce or an egg and butter liaison sauce. This dish, so simple to look at and to eat, is really quite difficult to achieve and you may have to practise it a couple of times before you manage the tricky bit of mixing the juices from the salt cod with the olive oil to form the thin custard-like sauce. It is worth the effort; it is a superb dish.

Serves 4

450g (1lb) salt cod, soaked for 24 hours
150ml (¼ pint) olive oil
4 cloves of garlic, chopped
2 tablespoons chopped fresh parsley
Freshly ground black pepper

Drain the salt cod and give it a rinse in some fresh water, then pat it dry with kitchen paper. Remove any obvious bones, but do not skin it.

Heat the oil in a large frying pan and sauté the chopped garlic for 2 or 3 minutes, until it is golden and smelling delicious. Scatter in the chopped parsley, stir it through and cook for another minute or so. Now use a slotted spoon to take the garlic and parsley out of the pan – just put them on one side for the time being.

Add the fish to the pan, skin side down, and cook over a very low heat for about half an hour, shaking the pan from time to time so the juices from the fish liaise with the oil to make a thin, custard-type sauce.

When you are ready to eat, pop the garlic and parsley back into the pan and cook for 2 more minutes. Add a few twists of ground black pepper (no salt!) and serve with the oil from the pan. It is the cod and garlic-flavoured olive oil that makes this dish. Boiled potatoes are the ideal accompaniment.

Tuna in Tomato Sauce

Atún en Salsa de Tomate

Serves 4

5 tablespoons olive oil
1 large onion, finely chopped
2 cloves of garlic, finely chopped
1 large green pepper, cored, seeded and chopped
4 × 225g (8oz) tuna steaks, about 2.5cm (1 inch) thick, skinned
Salt
300ml (1/2 pint) fresh tomato sauce (see page 13)
3 tablespoons fish stock
Freshly ground black pepper

Heat most of the oil in a frying pan and gently sauté the onion, garlic and pepper until softened and cooked – about 10–12 minutes altogether.

Meanwhile, pop the tuna steaks on to a grill pan and brush them with the remaining oil. Add a little salt, then grill them for about 10 minutes, until cooked, turning them once.

Quickly add the fresh tomato sauce and fish stock to the pepper and onion mixture and heat until it is bubbling. Reduce for a moment or two. Taste and adjust the seasoning if necessary. Place the fish on warm serving plates and pour over the sauce.

Delicious with sauté potatoes.

Eels in a Spicy Tomato Sauce

Anguilas en Salsa Picante de Tomate

The saltwater marshes in the north of Majorca are an area of outstanding beauty and tranquillity as well as home to thousands of birds. Narrow channels run between high walls of reeds, sometimes opening up to reveal a large lake, sometimes creating an aquatic maze.

A pal of mine, Miguel, has the good fortune of owning the only building for miles around on the edge of the water. He is a lawyer by trade but a hedonist by nature. Huntin', shootin', fishin', drinkin' and eatin' are what really thrill him. And every Saturday he and a dozen or so mates gather at his simple, white-washed, stone-floored lodge and shoot a few duck or teal or maybe the odd snipe. They then settle down to a day of cooking, eating, drinking and playing cards. (I have no doubt their wives are glad to see the back of them for that day.)

The marshes are teeming with eels, extremely popular food in this part of Majorca. Indeed, they even have an annual Eel Festival, at which great cauldrons of eels, vermicelli, potatoes, onions, carrots and broad beans are stewed over massive open wood fires. And there is music and dancing and, of course, eating and drinking. Needless to say, my visit to the island did not coincide with the Eel Festival. We, naturally, arrive at the wrong time, wherever we go. People always say, 'Ah, but you should have been here in the spring or the summer or the autumn.'

By way of compensation, Miguel punted me in his wooden craft through the eerie silence of the waterways. It reminded me of the Bayou in Louisiana except there were no crocodiles, alligators or racoons. But there were herons stalking, and water hens and ducks. When we peeked into the big lake, moving carefully so as not to cause a ripple or make a sound and disturb the birds, we made a slight splash and alerted what they call the 'alarm birds'. At the merest hint of a threat or intrusion of any kind, these birds take to the air. Perhaps a dozen or twenty of them wheel round and round above the other birds, squealing, squawking, shouting, ranting and raving to warn them to fly away. It was a spectacular sight to see maybe four or five thousand birds taking to the air at once.

Anyway, our main purpose was to go to the eel traps, ancient wicker baskets which Miguel places strategically round the marshes. We

hauled them up and got ourselves a bucketful of vibrant, wriggling eels. We then punted gently back to the lodge to cook them. It was quite one of the best meals I had on the entire trip.

Serves 4

900g (2lb) eels, cleaned and chopped into 5cm (2 inch) pieces
Salt
6 tablespoons olive oil
1 bay leaf
4 cloves of garlic, finely chopped
1 fresh green chilli pepper, seeded and finely chopped
1 large onion, finely chopped
6 medium tomatoes, skinned and finely chopped
2 small or 1 large leek, finely chopped
2 medium green peppers, cored, seeded and finely chopped
Freshly ground black pepper
A handful of chopped fresh parsley

Season the eels with a little salt. Heat half the oil in a frying pan and pop in the bay leaf, then add the garlic and chopped green chilli. Next, add the eels and stir them around, cooking them gently for approximately 10 minutes, until they are crispy. Lift out with a slotted spoon and put on one side – somewhere warm. Throw away the oil and all the bits – these were used just to flavour the eels.

Wipe out the pan and heat up the rest of the oil, then sauté the onion for a long, long time – until all water in it has evaporated. Next add the tomatoes, leeks and peppers and simmer them for a long time as well – about 35 minutes; this gives the strength of flavour that is characteristic of Spanish cooking. It really puts the sunshine into the dish. Tip in the eels and simmer very gently for 5 minutes, until they are warmed through and ready to eat. Check the seasoning and serve sprinkled with parsley.

Scallops in Shells
Coquilles St Jacques

Vieiras

For centuries pilgrims have been making their way to the Cathedral of St James at Santiago de Compostela, in the fond hope that such an arduous journey and the contrite embracing of the tomb would absolve them from their sins. (And pretty horrific sins they must have been in medieval times with rape and pillage, pinching neighbours' crops and cattle rustling.) It was not like present-day Lourdes where pilgrims go for physical cures.

Pilgrims still to this day wear as their talisman a scallop shell round their necks, which presumably were as plentiful then as they are now. Indeed, there were probably little food stalls all the way round the Cathedral selling scallops. After the pilgrims said their prayers in the Cathedral and begged forgiveness for their sins, they most likely had huge parties. It must have been enormous fun. You can imagine the great square in front of the Cathedral full of fortune-tellers, soothsayers and money-changers and pimps, prostitutes and gamblers, and stalls selling seafood and barrels of wine.

At night they would sleep in the huge galleries round the Cathedral. As sanitary conditions were non-existent and the pilgrims smelt pretty strong, the priests rigged up this giant ornate brazier that they filled with incense and herbs. They set fire to it and hoisted it up on a great rope and swung it dramatically in a huge, flaming, thunderous arc across the Cathedral to negate the awful smell of the pilgrims.

On the day I watched this ancient custom, I stood absolutely petrified. It could have been a scene from *The Omen* or Edgar Allan Poe's *Pit and the Pendulum*. Only four times has this flaming machine parted company from the rope and incredibly no one has been killed. But on one famous occasion it crashed at the feet of Catherine of Aragon, just before she was to be married to Henry VIII. That was an omen if ever I recognised one.

Serves 4

12 scallops in their shells
3 tablespoons olive oil
1 onion, peeled and finely chopped
1 clove of garlic, finely chopped
1 wineglass dry white wine
3 tablespoons aguardiente *or brandy*
1 teaspoon paprika
Pinch of cayenne pepper
Pinch of cinnamon
Salt
Freshly ground black pepper
4 heaped tablespoons fresh white breadcrumbs
Few knobs of butter

Split the scallops open with a sharp knife – go easy as you separate the two shells. The juicy edible parts are the white muscle and the pink coral. Chuck the rest away, apart from the shells.

Clean four of the shells, oil them lightly and divide the white parts of the scallop between them. Place these on a baking tray.

Heat the oil in a frying pan and sauté the onion and garlic for a couple of minutes until softened, then pour in the wine and *aguardiente* or brandy. Add the spices, pop in the corals and give everything a good stir. Cook for about 10 minutes or so, bubbling the sauce to reduce it. Taste and season.

Pour this sauce over the prepared shells and scatter the breadcrumbs on top. Pop a knob of butter on each and bake in a very hot oven, 200°C/400°F (gas mark 6), for about 10 minutes – and maybe put under a hot grill to brown the crumbs.

Prawns in Sherry Sauce

Langostinos al Jerez

Nursing a monstrous hangover, which was brought about not only by too much Málaga wine but also by the discordant jangling of 'authentic' Spanish flamenco dancing and music, the great guitarist John 'Fingers' Williams and I were painfully trying to come to terms with another splendid Spanish morning.

From a hotel terrace high above Málaga, we could see the Roman bullring and the busy port with lighters, cargo vessels, fishing boats and cruise ships. John was plucking away in between showers and squalls while I was trying to prepare him a little snack by way of saying 'Thank You' for contributing music to the programme. John Williams is really quite good, you know, and played the *Recuerdos de la Alhambra* by Tarrega with absolute brilliance, but his *Apache* wasn't up to much.

Anyway, this dish is dedicated to John Williams, the sort of kind, gentle and talented person you feel privileged to work with.

Serves 4

1 tablespoon olive oil
25g (1oz) butter
450g (1lb) large prawns – leave the shell just on the tail and the last joint
50g (2oz) serrano *ham, finely diced*
1 tablespoon chopped fresh parsley
60ml (2fl oz) dry sherry
Chopped fresh parsley, to garnish

For the sauce

25g (1oz) butter
25g (1oz) plain flour
150ml (1/4 pint) milk
150ml (1/4 pint) fish stock
1 level teaspoon Dijon-style mustard
Salt
Freshly ground black pepper

Make a simple white sauce of butter, flour, milk, fish stock and mustard. You know how, just melt the butter in a pan and stir in the flour to make a *roux*. Cook gently for a minute, then gradually add the milk and fish stock and finally the mustard, stirring all the time. Cook until the sauce has thickened and is smooth. (If you have a history of making lumpy sauces, try putting everything into a pan at once and bringing it up to the boil while you stir it non-stop with a whisk. I guarantee you a 'lumpless' sauce.) Check the seasoning to make sure it tastes good. Put to one side.

Next, put the oil and butter into an earthenware cooking pot (see page 203) or frying pan and heat until nearly smoking. Throw in the prepared prawns, ham and parsley and stir over a fierce heat for about 2 minutes. Whack in the sherry and bubble for 2 more minutes or so, stirring and turning the ingredients, then remove them from the heat and keep warm. Pour the juices into the sauce and heat through. Pour the sauce over the prawns, sprinkle with parsley and serve at once with crispy bread and a crunchy salad. Quick, easy and very tasty.

When you are parachuted, metaphorically speaking of course, into a strange town in a foreign country for the first time ever, it is difficult to see the gastronomic wood from the delicious trees. I had only been in San Sebastián in the Basque Country, on the north coast of Spain, for twenty-four hours, and as we were whirled round by a well-intentioned representative from the Tourist Board whose idea of good food had more to do with the decor and ambience than the stuff that appeared on the plate itself, I was beginning to worry that we would not get to the heart of the matter in the short time we had to spend there. But while buying some knives in a kitchen shop I fell into conversation with a genuine Basque person (as opposed to the professional Basque people the Tourist Board kept coming up with), who confirmed my suspicions of the Tourist Board's choice. He suggested some alternatives, one of which was José Juan Castilla's joint in the Calle Aldemar, beside the market in the centre of San Sebastián.

Unintroduced, at ten to twelve I knocked on his locked restaurant door, which was of fine polished oak and right at the top of an imposing panelled flight of stairs and asked to speak to the chef/proprietor. I explained that I wanted to see some authentic Basque cooking and that the owner of the kitchen shop had recommended him to me.

'Would it be possible to come in?' I asked. Without hesitation, without checking my identity or credentials, José generously invited me in and took me straight to the kitchen where nine or ten young cooks were industriously and lovingly preparing lunch. At once I recognised a serious kitchen and, with what some would describe as outrageous audacity, I asked to film there.

He said, 'When?'

I said, 'Now.'

He said, 'Fine, no problem.'

At one preparation table, four youngsters were painstakingly cleaning a mountain of baby squid, carefully removing the little transparent open collar bone that passes for its skeleton, meticulously squeezing the ink into a container. In another corner, two cooks were boiling live spider crabs, then dextrously removing the succulent body meat.

When we arrived I noticed the thermometer on the kitchen wall read 26°C. By the time Steve had put his lights up and we had switched off the extractor fans so Tim could record some clear sound, it had soared up to 40°C. But I had begun to discover that the Spanish have such a sense of hospitality and generosity that there was not a murmur of protest or query at working under these outrageous conditions. The only time there was a slight hint of reproof was not when we ordered them around and not when we told them to unplug their telephone lest it should ring during the take. Neither was it when we made them stand in uncomfortable positions nor when we cut off the communication system between the dining room and the kitchen. No, no, not at all; it only came when, after having completely knocked them out of sync for two hours during the busiest part of the day, we said we were too busy to stay for lunch.

Here beginneth the recipes. I am dictating this to Anne while sitting in the dining room of a totally nondescript hotel – we could be in Wigan Posthouse, if there is one, or in any Hilton or four-star hotel in the world. And yet as I speak, I am being served the finest lamb, simply roasted and served in its own juices, that I can remember for a long, long time. Apart from Anne's notepad, on the neatly-laid table there is a slightly green-hued bottle of mineral water, a Duralex glass bowl filled with crunchy lettuce, sweet slivers of white onion freshly tossed in olive oil, salt and vinegar, a couple of splendid bread rolls, an excellent bottle of *rosado* wine called Viña Arkupe from Rioja. But apologies, I got carried away. Here are the three recipes.

Kidneys a la JJ Castilla

Riñones a la JJ de Castilla

Serves 4

2 calf's kidneys – weighing about 675g (1½lb)
1 teaspoon chopped fresh thyme
Celery salt
Freshly ground black pepper
6 rashers of bacon
4 tablespoons olive oil
A little plain flour
150ml (¼ pint) good beef stock
1 sherry glass dry sherry or Madeira

Snip the core from the kidneys, along with any fat or membrane. Rinse them well and dry with kitchen paper. Season with the thyme, celery salt and pepper. Wrap three bacon rashers round each kidney, securing them with skewers.

Now heat the oil in a large frying pan. Pop the kidneys into the hot oil and seal them on both sides for a couple of minutes. Transfer them to a roasting tin and cook them in a preheated oven, 200°C/400°F (gas mark 6), for about 15 minutes, by which time the kidneys will still be pink (rare enthusiasts will enjoy this dish).

In the meantime, stir the flour into the oil left in the pan, cook gently for 1 minute, then gradually stir in the beef stock and heat until it has bubbled and thickened. Pour in the glass of sherry or Madeira and stir the sauce well.

When the kidneys have cooked, strain the juices into the sauce to give a richer flavour. Season to taste. Serve the kidneys with a few sauté potatoes and some whole, grilled tomatoes. Remove the skewers and pour over the sauce.

Baby Squid in its Own Ink (Squink)

Calamares en su Tinta

Serves 4

1.5kg (3½lb) baby squid, cleaned and prepared, see notes on page 205, with the ink sacs reserved
150ml (¼ pint) red wine
4 tablespoons olive oil
1 large onion, finely chopped
4 cloves of garlic, crushed
300ml (½ pint) fish or chicken stock
2 slices of bread, cut into chunks
Salt
Freshly ground black pepper
Plenty of chopped fresh parsley

Put the ink sacs into a sieve over a bowl and press them with a wooden spoon to extract the ink. Pour half the wine through the sieve to remove more of the ink – in fact, pass this liquid through the sieve two or three times to get as much ink out of the sacs as possible.

Chop the tentacles and fins, leaving the squid hoods or pouches in one piece. Heat the oil in a large frying pan and sauté together the onion and garlic, until they are softened and fragrant. Use about half this mixture to stir into the chopped tentacles and fins, then stuff it all into the squid pouches and secure with wooden cocktail sticks.

Pour the remaining wine into the frying pan with the onion and garlic that is still there, and add the fish or chicken stock. Pop in the ink mixture, add chunks of bread to thicken and season with salt and pepper. Add the stuffed squid and cook, covered, for about 2 hours over a very low heat, adding a splash of water to the pan if it threatens to boil dry. It will look like tar. Serve the squid on warmed plates with mounds of plain, boiled rice, sprinkled with parsley and with the fishy, chocolatey sauce.

Gratin of Spider Crab

Centollo Gratinado

Serves 4

4 spider crabs
4 tablespoons olive oil
1 medium onion, finely chopped
2 cloves of garlic, finely chopped
1 large leek, well washed and finely chopped
3 medium tomatoes, skinned and chopped
1 dessertspoon tomato purée
1 teaspoon paprika
Splash of dry sherry
Salt
Freshly ground black pepper
2 tablespoons fresh white breadcrumbs
A few knobs of butter

Boil the crabs in water for 15 minutes. Meanwhile, heat the oil in a large saucepan and sweat the onion, garlic and leek for about 10 minutes.

Remove the crabs from the boiling water and put on one side, upside down, until they are cool enough to handle. Then remove and discard the long, spindly legs and crack the bodies open to remove the crab meat.

Add the tomatoes, tomato purée, paprika and dry sherry to the onion mixture in the pan and season with salt and pepper. Simmer for about 15 minutes.

Mix together all the white and dark bits of the crab and add to the sauce. Mix well, then divide between shallow ovenproof dishes or the empty crab shells, which you have cleaned out and washed. Cover each one with a sprinkling of breadcrumbs and knobs of butter, and put under a preheated hot grill to 'gratinate'.

Mussels and Clams in Tomato and Wine Sauce

Mejillones y Almejas en Salsa de Tomate y Vino Blanco

PHOTOGRAPH OPPOSITE PAGE 41

One bright blustery morning we toddled out of the harbour at O Grove in Galicia on an open fishing boat, *Silvana Os*, to harvest mussels from rickety wooden contraptions a bit like miniature oil rigs, from which are suspended loads of ropes that the mussels attach themselves to. And for those of you who like statistics, a local lad told me 90 per cent of Spain's mussels come from around this part of the Sunshine Coast and they take three years to mature to commercial standards. There are 520 platforms with hundreds of ropes on each and 120 kilos of mussels on each full rope.

To add some interest to the sketch, though, we decided to cook for Paco, the captain, and for his black dog, who ended up eating much of the offering, because Captain Paco was a bit of a Spanish chauvinist and said though my dish was okay it was not really spicy enough. Truth of the matter was he was overawed and tongue-tied by being famous for fifteen minutes on a television programme. Well, that's my story and I'm sticking to it.

Serves 6–8

3.5kg (4lb) mussels
450g (1lb) baby clams (if you can get them)
150ml (5fl oz) olive oil
900g (2lb) onions, sliced
6 cloves of garlic, chopped into hefty chunks
2 bay leaves
2 tablespoons paprika
2–3 generous wineglasses dry white wine – I used Casal Caeiro
900ml (30fl oz) fresh tomato sauce –
purée about 2.5kg (3lb) skinned, seeded tomatoes in your blender, or use canned if you're pushed
Salt
Freshly ground black pepper
Lots of freshly chopped parsley, to garnish

First, find a pan big enough to take all the ingredients that has a lid. Scrub the mussels and clams well (or find a lackey to do it for you) and remove their black beards – the mussels', not the lackey's. Throw out any that are broken or that do not close when handled.

Meanwhile, heat the oil in the pan, add the onions and garlic and fry for a couple of minutes, giving them a good stir. Put on the lid and let the onions sweat it out for about 20 minutes.

Now chuck all the remaining ingredients into the pot and stir. Cover and bring to the boil, shaking the pan a couple of times to redistribute the mussels and clams. Cook for 2–3 minutes more, by which time all the shells should have opened. If any don't, throw them away.

Serve at once in bowls, with plenty of chopped parsley sprinkled over the top. Give your guests lots of fresh, crusty bread to mop up all the wonderful juices.

Clams in Tomato and Lots of White Wine

Almejas con Tomate y Vino Blanco

We were staying at a parador in a scruffy little Galician town that smelt and was full of half-finished breeze-block buildings. And although it was fiesta-time, there didn't seem to be a lot going on and, quite honestly, I didn't like the place, nor was the parador quite what I had been led to believe it might be.

So, feeling slightly disgrunted, Anne (my sort-of assistant-type person, who helps me write these books and accompanies me on my travels) and I set off into town looking for some simple food to eat. We found a place that had things like *huevos con jamón* (you know, ham and eggs, a dish which, by the way, the Spanish do particularly well as a rule) because it was one of those days when we'd had rather enough of rich stews and fine shellfish dishes and wanted something terribly straightforward.

But we were disappointed to find that whereas we could have ham and chips or eggs and ham, the café couldn't or wouldn't serve us ham, egg and chips. We were a bit miffed and decided to award Cambados about 3/10: to misquote the *Michelin* guide it is certainly not worth a detour. We then hopped a few miles up the coast to

O Grove and I still couldn't shake off the feeling that I had forgotten something – apart from my empty stomach.

It was 14th July. I soon remembered why the date rang a bell, it didn't take long. For the French it may be Bastille Day, but for me it was the first anniversary of the opening of my pub, The Maltsters Arms, in Devon.

So we drank a toast and polished off a plate or two of these delicacies, which more than made up for the disappointment of Cambados.

Serves 4

24 small clams in their shells
3 tablespoons olive oil
1 medium onion, finely chopped
3 cloves of garlic, finely chopped
4 large tomatoes, skinned and chopped
1 bay leaf
2 tablespoons chopped fresh parsley
25g (1oz) plain flour
2 teaspoons paprika
2–3 wineglasses dry white wine
Salt
Freshly ground black pepper

Put the clams in a colander and run them under the cold tap, throwing out any damaged ones. Drain them well.

Heat the oil in a large frying pan that has a lid and fry together the onion and garlic for a couple of minutes. Throw in the tomatoes, bay leaf and most of the parsley, cover and allow to 'sweat' for 5 minutes.

Add the clams and cook over a medium heat until they open. Sprinkle in the flour and paprika and stir well, then pour in the wine and add a good seasoning of salt and pepper. Continue cooking and stirring for another 5 minutes, remove the bay leaf, then serve.

Opposite: ***Above*** Chicken Stuffed with Raisins and Apricots (page 90), with Pickled Lemons and Limes (page 15); ***Below*** Lemon Chicken Sautéed with Garlic (page 87) *Next page, clockwise from top:* Rabbit with Red Peppers (page 97); Almagro Partridge (page 96); Granada-Style Chicken (page 82)

Mussels Vinaigrette

Mejillones en Escabeche

Serves 4

1kg (2¼lb) mussels, prepared for the pot (washed, scraped and beards removed – sounds like my early morning ritual)
1 clove of garlic, finely chopped
1 glass dry sherry (that's a sherry glass)
60ml (2fl oz) cold water
Salt
3 tablespoons olive oil
1½ tablespoons wine vinegar
1 dessertspoon chopped onion
1 dessertspoon chopped canned red pimientos
1 dessertspoon chopped fresh parsley
Freshly ground black pepper

Put the mussels into a shallow pan, which has a lid, with the garlic, sherry, water and a little salt. Switch the heat on high, pop on the lid and bring everything up to bubbling point. The mussels are ready to eat when they open up – take them out as they do so that they don't toughen. Chuck out any that refuse to open.

To make the vinaigrette: mix together all the other ingredients, including some salt, in a bowl. Taste to check the seasoning and if it is okay (it will be) pour over the mussels.

You should eat these with some fresh crusty bread to soak up the delicious juices.

Lobster with Chicken (page 74)

Lobster with Chicken

Langosta con Pollo

PHOTOGRAPH OPPOSITE PAGE 73

Serves 4

4 tablespoons olive oil
1.25kg (3lb) free-range, corn-fed chicken, jointed into small pieces like the Spanish do – see the note on page 83 (buy one with giblets and reserve the liver)
1 live lobster weighing about 1kg (2¼lb) – get your fishmonger to kill it for you if you're squeamish. Ask him to divide it into pieces, and remind him you need the green liver bit
1 medium onion, chopped
3 tablespoons brandy (but ideally aguardiente, grappa, *or* marc*)*
250ml (8fl oz) dry white wine
4 medium tomatoes, skinned and chopped
1 bay leaf
½ teaspoon fresh thyme
Pared zest of ½ orange
2 tablespoons chopped fresh parsley
2 cloves of garlic, crushed
75g (3oz) blanched almonds
75g (3oz) hazelnuts
1½ teaspoons grated dark chocolate
A few strands of saffron
300ml (½ pint) fish stock – this can be made by boiling the lobster's small claws and head in salted water for ½ an hour, or see page 16
Salt
Freshly ground black pepper

Heat the oil in a large frying pan. Pop in the chicken pieces and fry them quite briskly for 4 or 5 minutes, until nicely browned. Transfer them to a large casserole dish.

Now the lobster. Cook the tail and large claws in the same frying pan for a couple of minutes until pink, then lift out and put the pieces with the chicken.

Add the chopped onion to the pan and sauté until golden and well reduced, then stir in the brandy (*aguardiente* or whatever), wine, tomatoes, bay leaf, thyme, orange zest and 1 tablespoon of the parsley. Stir well and simmer gently for at least 15 minutes to reduce.

Stir this mixture into the casserole with the chicken and lobster and pop it into a preheated oven, 190°C/375°F (gas mark 5), for 10 minutes while you do the next bit.

You can either pound together the garlic, nuts, chocolate and saffron with the chicken and lobster livers in the time-honoured way or you can whizz together everything in a blender, adding a little fish stock to make a paste. However you do it, you must stir the results with the lobster and chicken in the casserole dish, adding the rest of the fish stock. Season with some salt and black pepper and leave to cook, covered, for another 15–20 minutes.

Fish out the orange zest, if it is still in one piece, and bay leaf. Garnish with the remaining chopped parsley and serve.

Garlic Prawns

Gambas al Ajillo

Serves 4 as a starter

450g (1lb) prawns, shells on
6 tablespoons olive oil
3 cloves of garlic, crushed
1 teaspoon cayenne pepper
2 tablespoons dry sherry
2 tablespoons lemon juice
Sea salt

Pat the prawns dry with kitchen paper. Heat the oil in a frying pan and sauté the garlic for a minute, then sprinkle in the cayenne pepper. Tip in the prawns and stir them well. Cook quite gently for 2–3 minutes, then spoon in the sherry and lemon juice. Stir through and serve at once, sprinkled with sea salt.

Poor Man's Lobster (Monkfish)

Langosta del Pobre

Goodness knows why this is called Poor Man's Lobster. Monkfish these days is a jolly expensive fish. The word *pobre* crops up on menus and place names all over Spain. I once lived in a village which was called Pobre Jesus, which means Poor Jesus.

Serves 4

675g (1½lb) monkfish, skinned and boned
2–3 cloves of garlic, very finely chopped
1 tablespoon paprika
Salt
Freshly ground black pepper
2 tablespoons olive oil
125ml (4fl oz) dry white wine (that is, 1 full wineglass)
Double cream and a knob of butter
Parmesan cheese

Rinse the monkfish and pat dry with kitchen paper, then cut into large chunks. In a large bowl, mix together the garlic and paprika with some salt and black pepper, then add a few drops of the oil. Chuck the fish into the bowl with this mixture, turning it over to coat it. Leave for about 20 minutes so that the flavours are absorbed.

Heat the oil – what's left of it – in a large saucepan. Add the chunks of fish, along with the seasonings, and cook for a couple of minutes, turning the fish pieces over to seal them.

Tip in the wine, cover and cook gently for 10 minutes (at the most), until the fish is done. Monkfish should be quite firm and not overcooked. When the fish is ready remove it from the pan and reduce the juices left in the pan to half their volume, using a little double cream and a knob of butter so you have a smooth creamy sauce. Pour it back over the monkfish pieces, sprinkle a little Parmesan cheese over the lot and pop it under a preheated grill to brown. And then you have a sort of Poor Man's Lobster Thermidor.

Bass in a Salt Crust

Lubina Salteado

Throughout Spain, in smart restaurants and beach bars alike, you will find a dish that is spectacularly visual, gastronomically perfect and yet so simple. It is a whole bass or bream baked in a block of salt. The success of the dish depends on the freshness of the fish.

The technique for preparing this dish is ancient and found in many cultures. Gypsies have put hedgehogs in clay and baked them over a fire. Maoris have dug pits in the sand, wrapped pigs and fish in banana leaves and cooked them over hot sticks. Chinese and Indians have used terracotta bricks. It is a straightforward method that doesn't allow any of the flavours of the principal ingredient to escape. And whatever you cook this way will be wonderful and not at all salty.

Serves 4

100g (4oz) softened butter
1 teaspoon chopped fresh tarragon
A small handful of fresh chopped parsley
3 cloves of garlic, chopped
Salt
Freshly ground black pepper
1 × 1.25kg (3lb) bass or bream, scaled, gutted and washed
2.75kg (6lb) coarse sea salt
Melted butter and wedges of lemon, to serve

Mix together the butter, tarragon, parsley, garlic, salt and pepper, adding the roe too if the fish has it. Stuff all this into the belly of the fish and sew up the opening.

Put a layer of salt in a big, deep casserole up to a depth of 3cm (1½ inches) and pop the fish on its back on top. Cover completely with the rest of the salt. Bake in a very hot preheated oven, 220°C/425°F (gas mark 7), for about 35 minutes.

Take care as you remove the casserole from your oven, as it will be very hot. Knock the bottom of the casserole if you need to, to loosen the salt block. Then carefully knock the salt from around the fish. Serve at once with the hot melted butter and lemon wedges.

POULTRY AND GAME

Chicken, Catalan-Style

Pollo a la Catalana

Irene España and her son Andrés Vidal, who run a hotel high up in the Pyrenees, were so taken by this dish that they decided to put it on the menu at their restaurant Casa Irena, which, incidentally, is favoured by the King, Juan Carlos. So who knows, by the time you read this, the King of Spain himself might have eaten one of my dishes.

Serves 4

6 tablespoons olive oil
1.25kg (3lb) free-range, corn-fed chicken, jointed into 4 pieces
1 onion, chopped
2 tomatoes, chopped
250ml (8fl oz) chicken stock
100g (4oz) stoned prunes
75g (3oz) raisins or sultanas
50g (2oz) pine nuts
25g (1oz) almonds, roasted
2 rich tea biscuits, crushed
1 wineglass dry white wine
Salt
Freshly ground black pepper

Heat half the oil in a large frying pan and pop in the chicken pieces. Fry them, turning over from time to time, until they are golden – about 10–15 minutes.

Meanwhile, heat the rest of the oil in a large saucepan and sauté the onion until softened – about 10 minutes. Stir in the chopped tomatoes and cook gently for 30 minutes, then pour in the chicken stock. Bring up to the boil, and bubble them together for about 20 minutes.

Go back to the frying pan and push the chicken joints to one side, then add the prunes, raisins or sultanas and pine nuts. Sizzle them together for about 3–4 minutes. Now strain in the onion and tomato sauce through a sieve. Lower the heat and simmer the lot for about 40 minutes.

Just before the end of cooking time, you need to make up a rather interesting paste with the almonds, biscuits and wine. This is called a *picada* in Spain, or a *pomade* in France, and it is used for thickening and flavouring. Grind down the nuts and biscuits, either with a mortar and pestle or in a grinder. Then mix them with the wine and stir into the other ingredients.

Heat together everything for a few moments, check the seasoning, then serve with something simple, like mashed or sauté potatoes. Wash down with a bottle of Marqués de Arienzo red Rioja 1985.

Chicken with Pine Nuts

Pollo con Piñones

Nuts are very popular in Spanish cooking. I remember the first time I had a chicken and nut dish. It was in the hills behind the coastal strip on the Costa Blanca in Alicante. And in an earth-floored wooden shack, doors open to allow some breeze to drift through the intense heat of the afternoon sun, I gorged myself on joints of free-range chicken that had been sautéed until golden and tender in olive oil with a little garlic and dozens of the sweetest, freshest almonds you could possibly imagine.

The almonds were not the sliced, dried, brittle things that you find in little cellophane bags in health stores. They were almonds plucked that morning from nearby trees; they had been split out of their soft, green outer shells and tossed into the pan just before the chicken was ready to serve. I think my hosts might have ground a bit of black pepper and sea salt over the chicken at the last minute and I seem to recall a hint of lemon – so, though I know that most of you could faithfully reconstruct the dish and flavour without any problems at all, here is a slightly more detailed recipe for a summer's day, involving pine nuts.

Serves 4

1.25–1.5kg (3–3½lb) free-range, corn-fed chicken, jointed into small pieces (see note on page 83)
50g (2oz) plain flour
4 tablespoons olive oil
1 onion, finely chopped
50g (2oz) serrano *ham, chopped*
2 cloves of garlic, crushed
1 wineglass dry white wine
120ml (4fl oz) chicken stock
50–75g (2–3oz) pine nuts
Fresh basil and parsley, chopped
1 bay leaf
Salt
Freshly ground black pepper

First, coat the chicken pieces in flour. Heat the oil in a casserole or large, heavy-based pan with a lid and fry the chicken until golden brown, about 4–5 minutes. Remove the chicken pieces with a draining spoon and put to one side while you throw the onion, ham and garlic into the pan.

Cook these together until the onion and garlic have softened – 2–3 minutes will do – then put the chicken back into the pot and stir in the wine and stock. Add your handful of pine nuts and herbs, a good pinch of salt and a few twists of freshly ground black pepper. Put on the lid and simmer for 45 minutes, until the chicken is tender. Remove the bay leaf before serving. Serve with Aubergine Fritters, see page 150.

Chicken with Orange and Mint

Pollo con Naranja y Menta

Serves 4

4 × 175g (6oz) boneless chicken breasts, skinned
Salt
Freshly ground black pepper
2 large knobs of butter
150ml (5fl oz) freshly squeezed orange juice
2 tablespoons chopped fresh mint
Sprigs of mint and orange slices, to garnish

Rub some salt and pepper into the chicken breasts to season them. Melt one of the butter knobs in a pan and sauté the chicken pieces for about 4 minutes, turning once. They should now be a light golden colour, and they will smell delicious.

Now pour in the orange juice, bring to a simmer, then cover and cook for 8 minutes or thereabouts. When the chicken is almost tender, throw in the chopped mint and stir it about a bit and whisk in the other knob of butter to thicken the sauce a little. Be careful not to overcook the chicken, or it will taste like cardboard.

Serve with some sautéed potatoes and a fresh green vegetable, not forgetting to garnish with some sprigs of mint and sliced orange.

Granada-Style Chicken

Gallinata Granadina

CENTRE-SPREAD PHOTOGRAPH BETWEEN PAGES 72 AND 73

This fascinating dish, literally translated as 'little hen from Granada', seems the sort of thing you would eat in a Persian restaurant, but it is as Spanish as flamenco dancing (though much better, I hasten to add).

In fact, it is a recipe in which the New World meets the Old. It shows how 500 years ago innovative Spanish cooks were quick to exploit the exciting produce coming out of the Americas, namely sweet potatoes, bananas and carrots.

Serves 4

3 tablespoons olive oil
1.5kg (3½lb) free-range, corn-fed chicken, jointed in the Spanish style (see page 83), into small pieces
4 cloves of garlic, peeled and finely chopped
2 medium onions, finely chopped
150ml (¼ pint) chicken stock
1 wineglass wine – dry white or rosado
2 cloves of garlic, peeled but not chopped
1 large carrot, or a couple of sweet potatoes, peeled and cut into chunks
2 bananas, peeled and cut into chunks
225g (8oz) fresh spinach, well washed and trimmed
Salt
Freshly ground black pepper
Fresh chopped parsley, to garnish

Put half the olive oil into a large frying pan. Heat it, then add the chicken pieces with the chopped garlic and onions. Cook for about 10 minutes until everything is golden. Add the chicken stock and tip in the wine. Let it bubble for a few minutes to reduce and evaporate the alcohol, then turn the heat to low, cover the pot and let it simmer for about 1–1¼ hours. (Check occasionally to make sure the pan doesn't boil dry.)

Meanwhile, in another pan, heat the rest of the olive oil. Add the other two cloves of (unchopped) garlic and cook for 2–3 minutes to flavour the oil. Remove the garlic, then add the carrot (or sweet potatoes) and cook for about 10 minutes over a low heat. Add the banana chunks and cook until they are a lovely golden brown.

At the same time, cook the spinach in a tiny amount of water for a few minutes, then drain it really well, squeezing out the excess moisture. Add this to the carrot and banana mixture and stir it through.

When the chicken is cooked, add the spinach and banana mixture. Let it all cook together for a few minutes, check the seasoning, then serve it, sprinkled liberally with chopped parsley.

PS This dish should be moist, but not too wet, if you get my drift.

Note

Many of the poultry recipes refer to the chicken being jointed in the Spanish style. The Spanish like to use the whole chicken, even the carcass, but it is all cut into bite-sized pieces with a chopper through the bone. They don't like to hack their way through great legs or huge breast joints. It is very much like the way the Chinese prepare their chickens. If you do prepare the chicken this way watch out for small bits of bone when you eat it.

Sunshine Roast Chicken with Vegetable Fritters

Pollo Asado con Verduras Rehogadas

Serves 4–6

1.25–1.5kg (3–3½lb) free-range, corn-fed chicken, with giblets
Sea salt
Juice of 1 lemon
2 tablespoons olive oil
6–8 cloves of garlic, unpeeled and roughly crushed

For the sauce

450g (1lb) very ripe, sweet tomatoes, skinned and seeded
2–3 tablespoons olive oil
1 fresh red or green chilli pepper, or both, seeded and finely chopped
2 cloves of garlic, crushed
2 shallots, finely chopped

For the fritters

Courgettes
Aubergines
6 tablespoons olive oil
Plain flour, for dredging
150ml (5fl oz) milk

Remove the giblets from the chicken and put them, with the chicken liver, into a roasting tray.

Wash the chicken well and pat dry with kitchen paper. Rub it, both inside and out, really well with sea salt and lemon juice, then rub oil all over. Place it, breast side down, on a rack over the roasting tray. Add the unpeeled crushed garlic to the giblets in the tray. Transfer to a preheated oven, 200°C/400°F (gas mark 6), and roast for about 1¼–1½ hours, until the chicken is tender and moist, but check with a skewer to see the juices run clear.

But you know as well as I do how long it takes to roast a chicken of that size in your oven, so as soon as you have popped it in, make this little sauce, which you will put into the tray underneath your chicken about 15 minutes before the chicken is cooked.

Put the tomatoes into a food processor or blender with the oil, chilli or chillies, garlic and shallots. Press the button and whizz it together so that you have a purée. Tip it into the roasting tray with the giblets and the juices that will have dripped from the chicken. As I said, do this 15 minutes before the end of cooking time. Stir it well, adding a splash of water if it is too thick.

After you have made the sauce, but long before you put it into the roasting tray, you must prepare your fritters. This is terribly simple to do. Cut the courgettes and aubergines into attractively-shaped thin slices, sprinkle them with salt and leave them for a while to draw out the moisture, then dry them with kitchen paper.

When the chicken is cooked, remove from the oven and let it rest for a couple of minutes while you finish the sauce. Bubble the contents of the roasting pan on the top of the stove, giving them a good stir. Check the seasoning and the texture, then strain through a sieve into a sauceboat.

Now the only complicated thing about this whole dish is the timing, because the fritters need to be cooked at the very last minute. Ask your loved one to give you a hand carving the chicken while you quickly cook the fritters. Heat the oil in a frying pan; dredge the vegetables in the flour, dip them into the milk and then fry them for a minute or two until golden, not burnt, on both sides.

By the time you have spooned some of the rich red sauce on to a white plate, placed some carefully carved slices of golden-brown chicken on top and arranged the green and purple golden fritters, you will see why I call this Sunshine Roast Chicken.

Chicken with Red Peppers

Pollo Chilindrón

This dish traditionally comes from Aragon in north-east Spain, an arid but dramatic and vividly coloured province. Great battles were fought there with the Moors in the Middle Ages. Anyway, this is not a history lesson, but an introduction to a delicious recipe for what some might call the ubiquitous chicken, to be found all over Spain.

Serves 4–6

4 tablespoons olive oil
1.5kg (3½lb) free-range, corn-fed chicken, jointed into small pieces like the Spanish do *(see page 83)*
3–4 cloves of garlic, roughly crushed
1 onion, chopped
75g (3oz) serrano *ham, diced (or you could use lean bacon)*
2–3 red peppers, cored, seeded and sliced into 1.25cm (½ inch) wide strips
450g (1lb) tomatoes, skinned, seeded and chopped (or be lazy and use a 397g [14oz] can chopped tomatoes, drained)
1 sprig of fresh thyme
1 bay leaf
Salt
Freshly ground black pepper
Chopped fresh parsley or coriander, to garnish

Heat the oil in a large shallow casserole or heavy-based pan that has a lid. Fry together the chicken pieces, garlic and onion for about 3–5 minutes until they begin to turn golden, then push them to one side of the pan. Add the ham (or bacon) and peppers and fry these for a minute or so until the peppers soften slightly, then stir everything in the pot together. Stand back and admire the brilliant colours.

Stir in the tomatoes, thyme and bay leaf, pop on the lid and simmer over a low heat for about 1½ hours, when the chicken will be tender and the sauce well reduced. Taste and add salt and freshly ground black pepper to your liking. Remove the bay leaf. Serve with rice or mashed potatoes, garnished with a sprinkling of parsley or coriander.

Lemon Chicken Sautéed with Garlic

Pollo Salteado con Limón y Ajo

PHOTOGRAPH OPPOSITE PAGE 72

Many visitors to Spain, unaccustomed to real Spanish cooking, often complain that the food is very greasy. True, there are badly-cooked greasy dishes in Spain as elsewhere. But the caring Spanish trencherman doesn't tolerate greasy food at all. Aromatically-flavoured oils with fish, chicken or meat can create the most subtle flavours. And this chicken dish, which relies for its excellence on the finest extra virgin olive oil, the freshest of herbs and the best possible free-range chicken, is one such delight.

Serves 4

1.5kg (3½lb) free-range, corn-fed chicken
50g (2oz) plain flour
4–5 tablespoons olive oil
12–16 cloves of garlic, roughly crushed
1 wineglass manzanilla fino *sherry*

For the marinade

4–5 cloves of garlic, crushed
Sprigs of fresh thyme, oregano and marjoram
Juice of 2 lemons or limes
Freshly ground black pepper

Okay, joint the chicken and cut into small bite-sized pieces. In a shallow dish marinate the pieces with a handful of crushed garlic, a bouquet of thyme, oregano and marjoram (these sweet herbs really do enhance the flavour of the marinade), the juice of a couple of lemons or limes and a few grinds of the pepper mill – and leave for at least 6 hours.

Now, using a slotted spoon, lift the chicken pieces from the marinade (reserving the marinade) and dredge them in the flour. Heat the oil in a pan and fry the pieces for about 5–8 minutes, until they are splendidly brown.

Add the cloves of roughly-crushed fresh garlic to the pot, allowing at least 3–4 cloves per person. When they have taken on a little colour, strain the marinade into the pot, add a very generous glass of *manzanilla fino*, and turn up the heat so that the oil, the sherry and the marinade bubble up. Then pop on the lid, reduce the heat and simmer for, say, 45 minutes, or until the chicken is tender and the sauce has evaporated, leaving mainly oil.

Serve the chicken and the garlic pieces on a warmed serving plate and pour over the aromatically-flavoured oil – the essence of this dish. This would be good served with sautéed potatoes and a salad.

PS By the way, I suggest you compare this dish with Hake with Potatoes and Garlic on page 46, which also uses aromatic oil.

PPS An interesting accompaniment to this dish, to give it that hint of Moorishness so often found in Spanish cooking, would be some Pickled Lemons or Limes, see page 15.

Chicken with Mushrooms

Pollo con Setas

If you had been a pilgrim coming through France, on foot, of course, or possibly by horse, donkey or pony, wearing your scallop shell as regular pilgrims did, you would probably have made the tortuous journey over the Navarre Pyrenees, on the north-east border of Spain. You would have stumbled down into the enclosed valleys, passed the stone houses with steeply pitched slate roofs, wandered through the Irati Forest, climbed over the limestone mountains, the Andei, the Urbassa et al, and dropped down to the Ebro basin and finally through the dense beech and pinewood forests.

And it is in these forests, or rather on the slopes of them, that to this day locals gather wild mushrooms in September and use them to make this tasty little dish, fit for peasant, pilgrim, poet or Pope. Use chanterelles, morels, ceps, whatever you can buy or whatever takes your fancy. This dish will happily feed four to six people if you cook a 3–4lb chicken, and though a pound of mushrooms would be fine, two pounds would be better and they can be assorted too.

Serves 4–6

5 tablespoons olive oil
1.25–1.8kg (3–4lb) free-range, corn-fed chicken, jointed in the Spanish way, into small pieces (see note on page 83)
6–8 cloves of garlic, crushed
1 liver, from the aforementioned chicken
450–900g (1–2lb) assorted mushrooms (chanterelles, morels, ceps, etc.)
Salt
Freshly ground black pepper
1 generous wineglass dry white wine

Heat the oil in a large frying pan and fry the chicken until golden brown, then transfer to a casserole.

Fry the garlic in the same pan for 2–3 minutes until tender, then add the chicken liver and lightly fry for 1 minute or so. Right, take the garlic and liver out of the pan and put to one side for a moment.

Now pop the mushrooms into the frying pan and sauté them until they are lightly cooked, about 2 minutes. Add them to the chicken in the casserole and season with salt and pepper.

For a really brilliant flavour, pour the wine into the frying pan that has the residue of the fried chicken, mushrooms and garlic and bubble it up, stirring well (this, as you all know, is called deglazing). Tip into the casserole over the chicken and mushrooms.

Go back to your chicken liver and garlic and whizz them together in your food processor or blender to make a paste, then stir this into the casserole. Put on the lid and cook over a low heat for about 1 hour, until the chicken is tender. This would be good served with Artichokes Braised in Wine, see page 139, and/or some baby new potatoes.

Chicken Stuffed with Raisins and Apricots

Capón relleno de Pasas y Albaricoques

PHOTOGRAPH OPPOSITE PAGE 72

For those of you who like to cook something really different without having to go to a huge amount of trouble or expense, here is a wonderful recipe to cheer up even the drabbest chicken. The sweet and sour chicken is simple to make and all you have to remember, to achieve success, is that your chicken will need at least three-quarters of an hour longer to roast because it is stuffed.

This is a typical Catalan dish that I cooked at the Barcelona Cookery School, where the enlightened local authorities are training young cooks to explore fully the Spanish culinary heritage and resurrect grand old dishes of former times.

Serves 4

1.25–1.5kg (3–3½lb) free-range, corn-fed chicken
Salt
50g (2oz) butter
225g (8oz) pork sausagemeat
100g (4oz) streaky bacon or pork, chopped
50g (2oz) dried apricots, soaked and chopped
50g (2oz) seedless raisins
50g (2oz) pine nuts
A handful of fresh white breadcrumbs
Freshly ground black pepper
2–3 tablespoons olive oil

Give the chicken a good rinse in some running water and pat it dry with kitchen paper. Rub some salt both inside and out.

Melt the butter in a pan and gently fry together the sausagemeat, bacon or pork, apricots, raisins and pine nuts for about 5–8 minutes. Mix in the fresh breadcrumbs and season with salt and pepper.

Use this mixture to stuff the cavity of the bird loosely – you must give room for the stuffing to expand a bit. Also, it is important that the heat can penetrate the chicken right through.

Immediately after you have stuffed the bird and stitched it up or secured it with skewers, baste it with the oil and bang it into a preheated hot oven, 200°C/400°F (gas mark 6), to roast for about 1¼–1½ hours, until it is tender and the juices run clear when the point of a sharp knife is inserted. You can put any spare stuffing into a little ovenproof dish and bake it at the same time.

Make some gravy to serve with the carved chicken from the roasting pan juices, some flour and a splash of dry white wine. (If you cook a couple of root vegetables and the odd bone or two alongside the bird while it is roasting, you'll get more flavour in your gravy.)

Carve the chicken. Dig out the stuffing and serve it alongside, with some roast potatoes, lots of vegetables and the delicious gravy.

Quail with Sultanas and Pine Nuts

Codorniz con Pasas de Esmirna y Piñones

CENTRE-SPREAD PHOTOGRAPH BETWEEN PAGES 104 AND 105

Serves 2

2 quail
2 tablespoons olive oil
Salt
Freshly ground black pepper
25g (1oz) butter
25g (1oz) pine nuts
50g (2oz) sultanas, soaked in a little hot water for an hour or two to plump them up, then drained
1 wineglass dry sherry

Rinse the quail and pat dry with kitchen paper, then rub over the oil and season with some salt and pepper. Put them on to a baking sheet or in a roasting pan and roast in a preheated oven, 190°C/375°F (gas mark 5), for 15–20 minutes, when they will look golden and delicious.

Just before the birds are ready, melt the butter in a small frying pan. Add the pine nuts and sultanas and sauté for about 3 minutes, until the pine nuts have turned a wonderful colour. Tip this lot over the quail, swiftly followed by the glass of sherry, which you ignite to flame the birds. Serve with a salad of winter leaves and game chips.

Duck with Olives

Pato con Aceitunas

CENTRE-SPREAD PHOTOGRAPH BETWEEN PAGES 104 AND 105

Serves 4

1 duck, weighing about 2kg (4½lb), quartered
(with giblets, if possible)
1 medium onion, sliced
2 cloves of garlic, finely sliced
5 tablespoons olive oil
500ml (16fl oz) dry white wine
100g (4oz) stoned, big green olives, roughly chopped
(buy Spanish ones if you can)
125ml (4fl oz) dry sherry
125ml (4fl oz) chicken stock – or duck stock if you want to make
it with duck's feet etc.
1 tablespoon chopped fresh parsley
½ teaspoon fresh thyme
1 bay leaf
A few black peppercorns
Salt

Make a few incisions into the duck quarters with a sharp knife and push in slivers of the onion and garlic. Pop the duck into a roasting pan with a couple of tablespoons of the oil and roast them in a pre-heated oven, 180°C/350°F (gas mark 4). If you have the duck giblets, roast these alongside, as they will help the flavour later. Half an hour in the oven should be plenty.

Transfer the duck pieces to a warm plate, then tip away the fat from the roasting pan, leaving giblets and juices. Now pour in half the wine and bring this to the boil on the top of the stove, stirring well to get all the wonderful flavours out of the roasting pan. (This, as you probably know, is called deglazing.) Use the rest of the wine to boil the olives in a small saucepan – 4 or 5 minutes will be fine, then drain them and put to one side.

Heat the remaining oil in a shallow flameproof casserole and fry the rest of the onion and garlic for 4 or 5 minutes, or until soft. Add the sherry, chicken stock, parsley, thyme, bay leaf, peppercorns and some salt. Pour in the deglazed pan juices and simmer for 5 minutes.

Pop the duck quarters into this pot, spooning over the sauce. Put on the lid and return to the oven for about 45 minutes more, adding the olives a few minutes before you're ready to serve, so they have the chance to heat through. Fish out the bay leaf before serving. Serve with game chips or crispy, roast potatoes.

Dallas Love's Partridge

Perdiz con Hierbas a la Dallas Love

You may have noticed that lovely recipe for Rabbit with Wild Mushrooms (see page 103). Well, my host for the day was a terrific woman called Dallas Love, who has been living up in the mountains with her horses, riding and trekking and observing the seasons come and go for many years. And because she had enjoyed my Rabbit with Wild Mushrooms, she invited me to her farm to cook this dish for me. Jolly good it was too.

Serves 2 if it's all you are eating, 4 if you are having a starter or a pudding

6 tablespoons olive oil
2 partridges, cleaned and chopped in half
4 tablespoons wine vinegar (red or white – it doesn't matter)
300ml (1/2 pint) good quality game or chicken stock
Freshly ground black pepper
Half-a-dozen whole cloves
2 cloves of garlic, chopped
Sprigs of fresh thyme
Sprigs of fresh rosemary
Salt

Heat the oil in a deep, flameproof casserole and brown the partridges on all sides. Add the vinegar and stock. Grind some black pepper into the cooking pot, then throw in the cloves, the chopped garlic and the fresh herbs. Sprinkle in a little salt, cover and simmer gently for about 1 1/2 hours. Serve with Potato Casserole, see page 154.

Partridge are plentiful in Spain, so if you liked the last recipe you could also try this one.

Partridge in Chocolate, Toledo-Style

Perdiz con Chocolate a la Toledana

Chocolate has been used in Spanish cooking since the discovery of the Americas, and though Partridge in Chocolate may sound strange to you it has an exquisite flavour. I had never cooked it before so my dearly beloved director found me a real-life Spanish Marquis to practise on. The Marqués de Griñón no less, who has an estate 50 kilometres or so west of Toledo, which is a magnificent town that has been pretty much ruined by souvenir shops selling imitation El Cid swords.

Like every self-respecting country estate, this one has a chapel attached to the house for the occasional family service. I don't think you can say you have really made it until you own a church or chapel. The house is surrounded by acres of carefully-tended vines and is found at the end of a 400-yard drive, the borders of which are thick with wild flowers, thyme and lavender, creating the appropriately rich scent that you would expect to inhale as you wandered around the estate of a *Marqués* with your 12-bore, rustic retainer and couple of gun dogs putting up the odd partridge of an early morning.

Add to that a thriving and innovative wine business, probably a small palace in Madrid, a beautiful wife and a British racing green Daimler, a wardrobe of well-cut clothes and hand-made shoes and you too would be extremely happy.

I have to say that the Marqués de Griñón – who happened to be the President of the Spanish Gastronomic Society, which made me a bit nervous having to cook for him I can tell you – is an absolutely smashing chap, urbane, charming, hospitable and friendly. And like only a real gentleman can, he put the crew and me at ease with generous glasses of wine, slivers of fine cheese and excellent ham. And what really made me warm to him was that he pronounced my finished dish a triumph.

His wines, by the way, are well worth drinking. We had *gran vino blanco seco* Marqués de Griñón 1989 D.O. Rueda and *gran vino tinto de crianza* Marqués de Griñón 1984.

Serves 4

2–4 partridges, cleaned and split in half
Salt
Freshly ground black pepper
3 tablespoons olive oil
1 medium onion, chopped
2 cloves of garlic, finely chopped
1 tablespoon plain flour
1 tablespoon wine vinegar
250ml (8fl oz) chicken or game stock
1 wineglass dry white wine
2 bay leaves
2 whole cloves
1 or 2 tablespoons grated dark chocolate (bitter is best)

Season the birds with some salt and black pepper. Heat the oil in a deep, flameproof casserole, add the partridge and fry them for 5 minutes or so to brown them on all sides. Add the onion and garlic and cook for 2–3 minutes more until they soften.

Now stir in the flour and mix well to make a *roux*, then add the vinegar, stock, wine, bay leaves and cloves. Bring it up to the boil and season with a little more salt and pepper.

Cover the pot and leave it to simmer for about 40 minutes, or until the birds are tender. Stir in the grated chocolate, mixing it in well, and cook for 15 minutes more, with the lid on. Remove the birds to a heated serving dish and strain the sauce through a fine sieve over them.

This tastes good with some plain boiled potatoes and a green salad.

Almagro Partridge (for Shaunagh)

Perdiz al Estilo de Almagro

CENTRE-SPREAD PHOTOGRAPH BETWEEN PAGES 72 AND 73

Red-legged partridge are plentiful in Spain and are not regarded as an expensive delicacy. In fact, in Toledo I had a partridge casserole with a dish of potatoes, sliced and baked in stock, for under a fiver.

The Spanish are a little naughty in their hunting and shooting habits. I must say I have no qualms about eating pheasant or partridge or whatever, which I feel are very much part of the food chain. But the Spanish shoot everything. Sparrows, thrushes, larks. Actually, they don't shoot them, they just send up such a hail of lead into the sky during the hunting season that the birds fly into it.

There is a recipe on page 94 for Partridge in Chocolate, but in stark contrast this one is served cold, a sort of potted partridge. It would make a splendid centrepiece for a grand picnic. I cooked it for my wife for just that reason; we stopped one hot day on the flat plains of La Mancha under the shade of some olive trees. We had a nice treat of *bocorones* – little fillets of fish marinated in vinegar – and a salad of really succulent big Spanish tomatoes simply dressed with salt and wine vinegar and olive oil. Incidentally, Spanish oils are mainly good ones and without parallel. We had a round huge country loaf cut into thick chunks, chilled wine and then wonderful cold partridge, followed by some slivers of Manchego ewes' cheese. And some ripe fresh peaches for dessert. It was a great day off, the next day we were back filming.

Serves 4

150ml (1/4 pint) olive oil
1 medium onion, chopped
2 cloves of garlic, chopped
2 bay leaves
4 partridge, cleaned, and chopped in half
250ml (8fl oz) dry white wine
2 whole cloves
8 black peppercorns
1 tablespoon salt
175ml (6fl oz) wine vinegar
10 strands of saffron

Heat the oil in a large, flameproof casserole and fry the onion lightly with the garlic and bay leaves, then add the partridge and cook for about 5 or 6 minutes, turning the birds from time to time, until they are browned.

Stir in the wine and sprinkle in the cloves, peppercorns and salt. Allow it to bubble and reduce for roughly 15 minutes, then add the wine vinegar. Let this boil for 5 minutes, then add 250ml (8fl oz) water and the saffron strands and cook gently for 1 hour.

These birds are delicious served cold. What you must do is skim any fat from the surface of the pot and refrigerate for 2 days before serving, turning each bird twice a day. Serve with the onion and garlic, and just a spoonful of the liquid. Watercress salad and cold apple purée go well with this, or serve it with some chutney.

Rabbit with Red Peppers

Conejo con Pimientos Morrones

CENTRE-SPREAD PHOTOGRAPH BETWEEN PAGES 72 AND 73

I thought my director had flipped his lid when he suggested a San Sebastián working men's club as the venue for a cooking sketch. I had visions of a set of *bains-marie* with tepid food sitting in them and a Perspex cabinet full of dried-out pies. And I felt no better when we actually arrived at the place, a large square room behind a plain brown door, filled with people playing cards or dominoes or sitting at a nondescript bar watching a television high on the wall. My heart sank even further when Pritchard said, 'Oh, by the way, you are actually cooking for eighteen of them.'

Earlier in the day I had decided to cook Rabbit with Red Peppers and had duly bought the ingredients at the market, but I couldn't really see this lot enjoying it – until, that is, I went downstairs to the kitchen. To my amazement, it had five or six different ranges and fifteen to twenty men were cheerfully and noisily cooking away for all the world as if it were the kitchen of a huge hotel. In fact, it was a cooking club and though women and children were admitted they were not permitted to cook. All the members of this club, be they lawyers or roadsweepers, make cooking their hobby and instead of playing golf or

joining the local flamenco dance group or the town band, they spend their spare time in the joyous art of cooking, eating and drinking. Any night of the week they prepare great feasts and the club's choral section sing with gusto rousing folk songs in praise of food.

Apparently, such clubs in Spain are peculiar to the Basque Country. It is an idea that should be universally adopted, particularly in Britain. Imagine all the pool halls and karaoke bars that could be turned into cookery clubs.

Like a great many dishes in Spain this one uses peppers and tomatoes. You can substitute the rabbit with meat or fish.

Serves 10

150ml (¼ pint) olive oil
450g (1lb) onions, chopped
900g (2lb) tomatoes, skinned and chopped
Sea salt
3 rabbits, each weighing about 1.25kg (3lb) and jointed into 6 pieces
8 cloves of garlic, chopped
Freshly ground black pepper
100g (4oz) serrano *ham, diced*
100g (4oz) chorizo, *diced*
900g (2lb) red peppers, cored, seeded and sliced into eighths
2–3 tablespoons chopped fresh parsley (or thyme or rosemary)

Heat half the oil in a very large saucepan (this will eventually take all the ingredients, so it needs to be big). Throw in the onions, stir well and sweat right down – this will take about 20 minutes. Add the tomatoes, plus a hefty pinch of sea salt and pop on the lid. Simmer gently while you get on with the next bit.

In another large pot heat the rest of the oil and add the rabbit pieces, sizzling and turning them for about 15 minutes, until they are nice and brown. Add the cloves of garlic and season with some black pepper. Stir well, then add the *serrano* ham and sausage. Now tip this lot into the pan with the onions and tomatoes, giving everything a good stir.

In the pot that you've just emptied, chuck in the sliced peppers, stirring them well. Cook them quite briskly in the oily residue for a few minutes until they have softened, then add them to the pot containing all the other ingredients. Sprinkle the parsley into the pan as well, and season with some more sea salt. Simmer gently for about 45 minutes, when you will have made the most wonderful rabbit stew.

Romesca Rabbit

Conejo Romesco

I first tasted this dish when my chum Francine was cooking it for ten to twelve people at her Restaurante Dida in Barcelona. She didn't bother to weigh or measure her ingredients very much, but I learnt two essential things about Spanish cooking from her, which apply to every recipe in this book where onions, tomatoes or *picadas* are used.

The first was her approach to cooking the onions. She had a great bowl of them finely chopped – about ten altogether – and she tipped them into about a litre or a half-litre of olive oil and patiently sweated them away until they were around one-quarter of their original volume and all the water had evaporated. It became almost a purée of golden onions.

Then she added a vast amount of skinned, chopped tomatoes to the onions and a bit more olive oil and sweated them down until they were about one-quarter of their original volume. This gave a real intensity of flavour. The process took three-quarters of an hour. Also, when Francine sautéed the rabbit in olive oil, she did so slowly.

Meanwhile, she used a pestle and mortar to grind every possible flavour out of the *picada* ingredients. So though the dish looks quick and easy, it will be much improved if you take Francine's tips that I have outlined here. It goes without saying, of course, that she used wonderful mountain rabbits, which had been munching on thyme and rosemary before they were collected for the pot.

Serves 6–8

6 tablespoons olive oil
2 onions, finely chopped
6 or 8 large tomatoes, skinned and finely chopped
1 clove of garlic, finely chopped
Small mound of chopped fresh parsley
2 rabbits, each weighing about 1 kg (2¼lb), jointed, livers reserved
Plain flour, for dusting the rabbit pieces
Salt
Freshly ground black pepper
Couple of wineglasses dry white wine
A bouquet garni – made from thyme, rosemary, a bay leaf and stick of celery
Pinch of paprika (optional)

For the picada

50–75g (2–3oz) toasted, ground hazelnuts
A good pinch of saffron strands
2 cloves of garlic, finely chopped
A dash of olive oil
2 or 3 dried red chilli peppers or one dried red pepper, chopped
Livers from the rabbits, precooked in olive oil

First, make a paste from the *picada* ingredients by either pounding them in a pestle and mortar or puréeing them in your kitchen blender. Put this smooth, rich paste to one side for the moment.

Now in a large frying pan heat some olive oil and sweat down the onions until they are one-quarter of their original volume. Then add the chopped tomatoes and some garlic and parsley and let that reduce until you have a thick, rich red sauce. Put to one side.

Dredge the rabbit pieces in flour and fry them gently in olive oil with the garlic and some salt and pepper, turning the bits frequently

until they are completely sealed. Add a couple of glasses of wine and the onion and tomato mixture. Pop in the bouquet garni, put a lid on your pan and simmer gently for about 40 minutes, or until the rabbit is almost cooked. If the dish looks a little dry, add a drop of chicken or game stock or, if the worst comes to the worst, a little water.

Add the *picada* and stir this in and simmer for another 10 minutes or so, until the sauce becomes really thick and flavoursome. It will be slightly spicy because of the chillies or the dried red pepper. If, like me, you like spicy things from time to time, you could add a pinch of hot paprika to emphasise this.

Stuffed Rabbit

Conejo Relleno

Rabbit is not a very popular dish in Britain, which is a pity because good country rabbit in a pie or stew is great. Many of the customers at my pub won't have rabbit because they don't like the bones in it. Well, when I was at the Barcelona Cookery School they showed me a scrumptious rabbit dish and for the little trouble it takes to remove the bones I am sure you will be delighted with it. If you haven't the confidence yourself to trim it neatly, ask the old butcher to do it.

For those of you who are health-conscious and concerned about cholesterol – unlike me – rabbit is absolutely perfect as it is one of the few meats that genuinely has flavour but no fat. So give it a whirl. In my book a finely-cooked, free-range rabbit knocks the pants off a piece of specially-bred pork that has neither fat nor crackling on it.

Serves 4

1 rabbit, weighing about 1.25kg (3lb), jointed and boned
1 large carrot, cut into julienne strips
100g (4oz) runner beans, cut into julienne strips
Liver and kidneys of the rabbit, diced
Salt
Freshly ground black pepper
150ml (¼ pint) olive oil
1–2 wineglasses dry white wine
Knob of butter

If your butcher hasn't boned the rabbit for you just scrape the meat away from the bones – it's quite easy with the rabbit already jointed.

Bash out the boned rabbit pieces, gently but firmly, with a meat mallet or rolling pin to flatten them. Stuff with a mixture of the finely cut vegetables and liver and kidney, and roll the rabbit around, securing each piece with a cocktail stick while you tie them up neatly with string. Take out the cocktail sticks. Season the rabbit with salt and pepper.

Heat the oil in a saucepan or flameproof casserole and pop in the rabbit. Put on the lid and cook gently for about 45 minutes, when the rabbit should be ready. Taste a piece, and if it is still slightly on the tough side cook for another 15–20 minutes or so.

Remove the rabbit pieces and keep warm. Deglaze the juices in the pan with a glass or two of dry white wine. Whisk in a knob of butter, season with salt and pepper and strain the sauce through a sieve over the rabbit.

Rabbit with Wild Mushrooms

Conejo con Setas Silvestres

The Sierra Nevada mountains above Bubión in the Alpujarras – a hilly, picturesque district not far from Granada – are spectacularly beautiful and on a clear day you can see North Africa across the shining Mediterranean Sea. But on the day we chose to do a little horse riding and wild mushroom hunting, snow clouds set in, visibility was down to a few hundred yards and it was minus 6 degrees – Celsius, of course. Even cantering around on a couple of mighty chargers did nothing to warm us up and my hands were numb with cold when I set up my trusty portable stove and cooked this warming, typical mountain sheep-farmers' dish.

Serves 4

1 rabbit, weighing about 1.25kg (3lb), jointed
3 tablespoons olive oil
2 medium onions, chopped
4 cloves of garlic, chopped
175g (6oz) serrano *ham, diced*
300ml (1/2 pint) red wine (or thereabouts)
Salt
Freshly ground black pepper
225g (8oz) wild mushrooms
(if you buy dried, soak them first), sliced

Rinse the rabbit pieces and pat dry with kitchen paper. Heat the oil in a flameproof casserole and add the rabbit, frying for about 4–5 minutes to brown and seal the pieces, then remove them and put to one side.

Sauté the onions and garlic for about 4–5 minutes until softened, then add the *serrano* ham. Cook for a couple of minutes, then put back the rabbit into the pan. Pour over the wine to cover. Season with some salt and pepper.

Simmer for 30–40 minutes, then if the rabbit is nearly done add the wild mushrooms, stirring well. Cook gently for another 10 minutes, then serve. Tastes good with mountains of mashed potato.

Hare with Brown Lentils

Liebre con Lentejas

Serves 4

350g (12oz) washed and rinsed brown lentils, soaked for at least 3 hours in 600ml (1 pint) good stock
1 hare, weighing about 1.25–1.5kg (3–3½lb), jointed and marinated in 150ml (¼ pint) dry white wine for the same amount of time
3 tablespoons wine vinegar
1 bay leaf
Half-a-dozen peppercorns
2 tablespoons olive oil
1 medium onion, chopped
2 cloves of garlic, chopped
1 red pepper, cored, seeded and chopped
1 fresh red (you could use green) chilli pepper, seeded and finely chopped
2 medium tomatoes, skinned and chopped
Salt
Freshly ground black pepper

Put the lentils with the stock into a very large, flameproof pot with a lid. Drain the hare and add the pieces to the pot. Add the wine vinegar, pop in the bay leaf and peppercorns and put on the lid. Simmer for about 1 hour while you watch a video of *Floyd on Oz*.

Come back to heat the oil in a frying pan and sizzle together the onion, garlic, red pepper, chilli pepper, tomatoes and seasoning. After they have cooked for about 5 minutes, tip them into a food processor or blender and whizz until they are smooth.

Stir this blended mixture into the large cooking pot with the hare and lentils and continue to bubble away gently until everything is deliciously tender – it will take about another half an hour. Taste and adjust the seasoning if necessary. Delicious with rice, or potatoes if you prefer, and perhaps a salad. A robust red wine goes well with this.

Opposite: Empanada (page 123)
Next page, clockwise from top: Rabbit with Pears and Turnips (page 105); Duck with Olives (page 92); Quail with Sultanas and Pine Nuts (page 91)

Rabbit with Pears and Turnips

Conejo con Peras y Nabos

CENTRE-SPREAD PHOTOGRAPH BETWEEN PAGES 104 AND 105

I have included this dish because of the fascinating combination of ingredients, namely rabbit and pears. A simple rabbit stew with carrots, onions and turnips – little baby ones, nicely peeled – cooked in stock would be a nice English way to prepare this. But the addition of pears and a drop of white wine lifts it out of the ordinary and into the exotic and amusing.

Serves 4

1 rabbit, weighing about 1.25kg (3lb), jointed in the Spanish style – see page 83
2 tablespoons plain flour
Salt
Freshly ground black pepper
250ml (8fl oz) olive oil
½ wineglass brandy
1 wineglass dry white wine
250ml (8fl oz) chicken or rabbit stock or water
1 large onion, chopped
2 cloves of garlic, chopped
1 large carrot, roughly chopped
4 turnips, roughly chopped
1 leek, sliced
4 large pears, cored and quartered (do not peel)
1 ripe tomato, skinned and chopped
A small bundle of fresh herbs – for example, thyme, rosemary, parsley and a bay leaf

Roll the pieces of rabbit in the flour, which you have seasoned with some salt and pepper. Heat half the oil in a large flameproof casserole and fry the rabbit for about 10 minutes, until it is golden brown. Pour in the brandy and set fire to it with a match. When the flames have

Oxtail Stew (page 137)

died down, pour in the wine and stock or water. Bubble away gently while you carry on in another pan.

Heat the rest of the oil and fry the onion, garlic, carrot, turnips, leek and two of the pears. When they are soft – about 8–10 minutes – pop in the tomato and bouquet garni. Tip this lot over the rabbit and carry on cooking, adding more liquid as it is needed, until the rabbit is really tender – about 1¼ hours should be fine. Ten minutes before serving, add the remaining two pears.

Rice and Meat Hotpot

Arroz Brut

Palma, Majorca, is a fine holiday town and it is great for burgers, Cuba Libres and fast food. It has a spectacular cathedral and wonderful harbour. But you need to venture out a bit to find the authentic Majorcan cooking.

The barman at the Valparaiso Hotel recommended that we go to a little village called Genova, which has a handful of good Majorcan restaurants. We chose one quite arbitrarily, Restaurante Llompart, and sat for twenty minutes or so eating olives and sipping sherry, watching what the locals were eating.

There were wonderful whole legs of roast lamb, rabbit fried with garlic, aubergines stuffed with tomato sauce and splendid, crunchy green salads. But the speciality appeared to be a cross between a paella and a jambalaya; a wonderful dish, half soup, half stew, of meat, rice and snails. And with the aid of my brilliant Spanish, I stumbled, bloated and happy, into the kitchen and made friends with Isabel, the cook/patron. I chatted her into letting us film her kitchen then and there. This was a remarkable achievement because I don't, in fact, speak any Spanish, and she no English. But I understood enough to be able to reproduce the dish faithfully here.

Serves 4

8 tablespoons olive oil
900g (2lb) mixture of rabbit, chicken and pork, cut into bite-sized pieces
1 large onion, chopped
1 green pepper, cored, seeded and chopped
2 large ripe tomatoes, skinned and chopped
Salt
Freshly ground black pepper
50g (2oz) peas
50g (2oz) green beans, sliced
100g (4oz) butter beans, cooked (canned will do)
1 red pepper, cored, seeded and chopped
50g (2oz) wild mushrooms, chopped
8 snails, if you like them
Few strands of saffron
350g (12oz) long-grain rice
450ml (3/4 pint) chicken stock
Fresh chopped parsley and finely chopped garlic, to garnish
Slices of green pepper and lemon wedges, to serve

Heat the oil in a large casserole and pop in all the meat, frying it gently for a good 10 minutes to brown it. Chuck in the onion, green pepper and tomatoes, plus a little salt and pepper. Cook for about 10 minutes.

Next, add more *verduras* – peas, green and butter beans, red pepper and wild mushrooms. Pop in the snails if you're using them and add the saffron strands. Tip in the rice and add the chicken stock, then bring to the boil and simmer until tender – about 20 minutes, when the moisture should have been absorbed.

Ladle the food on to warmed serving plates and sprinkle with parsley and garlic. Serve with a side dish of raw green pepper slices and a wedge or two of lemon.

Meat

Pot Roast Shin of Beef

Puchero de Jarretes de Vaca Asados

When my friend Moncho Vilas, of the Restaurante Casa Vilas in Santiago, told me about this dish I felt it had little chance of tasting good. But despite its short list of unprepossessing ingredients, it turned out to be a very fine dish indeed, not dissimiliar to the kind of *estouffades* or stews favoured by the French cowboys in the Camargue.

The secret of the dish is to brown the meat fiercely on all sides, to brown the onions so that they are quite caramelised, and to cook until the meat is very tender.

We served this dish to the President of Galicia as well as Salmon with Clams (see page 49) and he pronounced it extremely good. We washed it down with an interesting Galician red wine called Rectoral de Amandi, 1989.

Serves 4

900g (2lb) shin of beef, in one piece
Salt
Freshly ground black pepper
300ml (½ pint) dry white wine
4 cloves of garlic, crushed
6 tablespoons olive oil
8 onions, sliced (yes, the Spanish do like their onions)

Trim the fat from the shin of beef (Moncho left it on the outside, but I prefer to trim it off). Season with salt and pepper and marinate it in the white wine and garlic for at least 8 hours – overnight would be better. Turn the meat from time to time, but don't bother getting up in the middle of the night to do this.

Next, heat the oil in a pan so that it is all but smoking. Take the meat out of the marinade (save this for later) and plop it into the cooking pot, searing it well to brown on all sides. Keep the heat high to do this. Transfer the meat to a heavy casserole dish. Now brown the onions in the same oil as the beef, and when they're done tip them into the casserole with any oil left in the pan.

Pour over the marinade, pop on the lid and cook in a preheated oven, 160°C/325°F (gas mark 3), until the meat is truly tender, approximately $1^1/_2$ hours. This would be good served with Potatoes with Paprika, see page 154.

Beef and Potato Hotpot

Estofado a la Patatas

CENTRE-SPREAD PHOTOGRAPH BETWEEN PAGES 168 AND 169

I left Granada for the flat plains of La Mancha with great relief. We had stayed in the most appalling hotel close to the Alhambra Palace, complete with iron bedsteads, faulty lighting, cockroaches, surly staff and lousy food. Don't hesitate to write to me if you want to know the name of the place.

On the open rolling road, through miles and miles of olive groves, my spirits lifted. And as windmills began to appear on distant skylines, thoughts of Don Quixote and Sanchez started to occupy my imagination. This whole trip was a tilt at gastronomic windmills; sometimes we succeeded, sometimes we failed. One striking success was an arbitrary stop at a roadside filling station and restaurant-cum-café where I had a huge pot of potatoes stewed with saffron and little pieces of meat. For about £1 it was a friendly meal. We washed it down with a pleasant bottle of Valdepeñas, the local wine. By the way, Valdepeñas wines are extremely drinkable and we don't see enough of them in Britain where Rioja seems to be more available. They are light-tasting, though strong, and made from a mix of red and white grapes and drunk with little ageing; I recommend them to you wholeheartedly.

Anyway, full of terrific cheer we set off for the charming town of Almagro. This has an architectural gem in the shape of covered walkways – rather like the Buttermilk in Dartmouth – round the central square, which that day was a hive of activity as the worthies of the town council were taking delivery of a brand new red fire engine and everyone was having rides up and down in the hydraulic lift it had attached to it.

After a splendid night in a modern but terribly good hotel just on the outskirts of Almagro, I set up my trusty camping stove right in the middle of a vast vineyard and tried to recreate the *Estofado a la Patatas* that I had eaten at the transport café the day before.

Serves at least 8 hungry people

6 tablespoons olive oil
900g (2lb) stewing beef (or pork, or veal), cut into large chunks
300ml (½ pint) beef stock
2 medium onions, sliced
1 red pepper, cored, seeded and chopped
1 green pepper, cored, seeded and chopped
4 tomatoes, skinned and chopped
3–4 cloves of garlic, finely chopped
2 tablespoons paprika
900g or 1.25kg (2 or 3lb) potatoes, cut into large chunks
2 wineglasses dry white wine
large pinch of saffron strands
Salt
Freshly ground black pepper

Heat half the oil in a large, flameproof cooking pot. Chuck in the meat and keep the heat on high while you brown it well. Pour in the beef stock and bring to the boil. Reduce the heat, cover and cook until the meat is tender – about an hour and a half.

Meanwhile, start to cook the other ingredients. Heat the rest of the oil in a large saucepan and add the onions with the peppers, tomatoes, garlic and paprika. Sauté them together for a few moments, then leave them to sweat it out for at least 30 minutes or so. Then add this sauce to the meat, pop in the potatoes, wine and saffron and simmer for about 15–20 minutes, until all are tender. If necessary, add a drop more beef stock if the dish looks too dry. Wash down with a glass or two of your favourite Spanish wine.

Beef Leftovers with Aubergines

Ropa Vieja de Carne de Vaca y Berenjenas

Serves 4

2 medium aubergines, sliced
Salt
5 tablespoons olive oil
1 medium onion, chopped
1 clove of garlic, finely chopped
1 dessertspoon plain flour
5 tablespoons beef stock
150ml (1/4 pint) fresh tomato sauce (see page 13)
2 canned pimientos, drained and sliced
450g (1lb) cooked beef, torn into thick shreds
Freshly ground black pepper

Lay the aubergine slices on a flat surface and sprinkle with salt. Leave them for about 15 minutes or so, turn the slices over and repeat the process. This brings out excess moisture. Do not rinse, just shake and pat dry.

Heat the oil in a large frying pan and sauté the aubergine slices quite briskly to brown them. Remove from the pan and keep warm. Add the onion and garlic and fry for 3 or 4 minutes, until softened and beginning to brown.

Stir in the flour and cook gently for 2 minutes, then add the stock and tomato sauce, bringing the mixture to the boil to bubble and thicken. Add the chopped pimientos and return the aubergines to the pan. Simmer for 5 minutes, then add the cooked beef. Keep simmering for another 5 minutes to heat through, season with salt and pepper and serve at once.

Note

Onions should be sweated down for a long, long time, until all the water in them has evaporated. Then the tomatoes should be simmered for a long time. This gives the strength of flavour that is characteristic of Spanish cooking. It really puts the sunshine into the dish.

Beef Stew with Garlic and Prunes

Guiso de Carne de Vaca con Ajos y Ciruelas

My assistant Anne and I, shattered, stopped for lunch in a dusty, unkempt village on a busy main road that was overshadowed by a cathedral or perhaps a monastery on the top of the hill behind. We had just had the most exhilarating drive over the Spanish Pyrenees, skipping across the roof of the world in an open-topped car. Massive vistas, empty roads, terrifying bends, precipitous descents, the sun high in the big blue sky. Anyway, I was wrecked as I had been doing all the driving since I didn't trust Anne on the bends because she drives faster than me. So we fell into this restaurant absolutely starving. And this was the brilliant meal we had, a rather English beef stew of garlic and prunes, which was served with a rice salad.

Serves 4–6

2 tablespoons olive oil
900g (2lb) stewing beef, cubed – with some fat on the meat
At least 6 cloves of garlic, peeled and roughly chopped
1 onion, chopped
½ teaspoon cornflour
1 wineglass dry white wine
175g (6oz) tomatoes, skinned and chopped
3 whole cloves
1 large bay leaf
1 teaspoon chopped fresh thyme
1 teaspoon chopped fresh oregano
1 tablespoon chopped fresh parsley
3 large potatoes, peeled and cut into chunks
225g (8oz) prunes, stoned
Salt
Freshly ground black pepper

Heat the oil in a large cooking pot. Chuck in the meat and brown it, keeping the heat on high, then turn it down and add the garlic and onion. Cook for about 4–5 minutes, until they soften.

Mix the cornflour with the wine and add to the meat, stirring well until it thickens slightly. Add all the other ingredients apart from the potatoes and prunes. Simmer, with the lid on, for about $1^3/_4$ hours, until the meat is tender (but not falling apart).

While it is cooking, and when it suits you, parboil the potatoes for 10 minutes. In a separate pan, simmer the prunes in a little water for about 10–12 minutes to swell them up.

When the meat is almost ready, pop in the potatoes and cook for 10 more minutes. Finally, you add the drained prunes and cook just long enough to heat them through. This way the prunes keep their distinctive flavour and don't get swallowed up by the stew. Season to taste.

Braised Leg of Lamb with White Beans

Pata de Cordero Cocida a Fuego Lento y Alubias Blancas

Serves 4–6

225g (8oz) white beans, such as haricot or butter beans, soaked overnight
Salt
Freshly ground black pepper
1 × 1.25–1.5kg (3–$3^1/_2$lb) leg of lamb, boned, rolled and tied
4 tablespoons olive oil
6 small onions, quartered
4 cloves of garlic, finely sliced
4 medium carrots, cut into chunks
500ml (16fl oz) beef, chicken or lamb stock

Drain the soaked beans and rinse them in some fresh water. Pop them into a large saucepan and cover with cold water. Bring them to the boil, then reduce the heat and cook for about 1 hour, seasoning halfway through. Don't forget to check the water level occasionally to prevent them from boiling dry.

Meanwhile, season the lamb with salt and pepper. Heat the oil in a large flameproof casserole dish and brown the rolled lamb gently, then add the onions, garlic and carrots, cooking them for a few minutes to brown them as well. Pour in the stock, then cover and simmer for about $1^1/_2$ hours, adding the drained, cooked beans after 1 hour. Cook until the lamb and beans are tender. A lovely rustic dish that tastes excellent just with some hunks of fresh, crusty bread.

Spiced Lamb

Tafalla Blanca

Serves 4

4 tablespoons olive oil
1 large onion, chopped
1 small bulb of garlic, broken up into cloves but not peeled
1 bay leaf
1.5kg ($3^1/_2$lb) boned shoulder of lamb, cut into chunks (ask your butcher to give you the bone – it will make excellent stock)
1 wineglass dry white wine
1 cinnamon stick
2 teaspoons ground cumin
2 teaspoons ground coriander
1 teaspoon ground nutmeg
1 teaspoon ground ginger
Salt
Freshly ground black pepper
25g (1oz) butter
100g (4oz) blanched almonds
2 tablespoons cornflour

Heat the oil in a large frying pan and fry together the onion, garlic and bay leaf for 5 minutes, or until the onion looks transparent. Add the lamb pieces, a handful at a time, frying these over a high heat to seal them. Cook for about 15 minutes, then pour in your glass of white wine, bubbling it for a minute or two to throw off the alcohol. Add enough water to cover and add the lamb bone, if you have one, to make the stock taste superb. Put all the spices into a large square of muslin and draw this up to make a little bag, then pop it into the stock. Season with salt and pepper.

Bring the stock to the boil, reduce the heat and simmer gently for approximately 2 hours, by which time the lamb should be very tender.

Melt the butter in a small pan and fry the almonds until golden, then chop finely. Add these to the pan 10 minutes before the end of cooking time. Fish out the bag of spices and the bay leaf, then thicken the sauce with the cornflour, blended with a little cold water. Check the seasoning and serve with vegetables, or chick peas or haricot beans.

Lamb with Almonds

Cordero Almendrado

At a glance, the ingredients for this delightful dish might make you wonder why Floyd has slipped an Indian recipe into a Spanish cook book, when you have only to add some chillies and a few more spices and you would have a jolly interesting curry. But, in fact, it is a Spanish dish that owes its origins to the Moorish occupation of Spain up to the Middle Ages. It was the Moors who had a taste for sweet and sour food – or perhaps one should more correctly say hot and sweet.

Serves 4

4 tablespoons olive oil
675g (1½lb) lean lamb, cut into chunks
500ml (16fl oz) lamb or vegetable stock
1 medium onion, peeled and roughly chopped
1 teaspoon coriander seeds, crushed
1 teaspoon fresh root ginger, chopped
175g (6oz) ground almonds
1 teaspoon ground cinnamon
Freshly ground black pepper
Salt
4 eggs, hard-boiled and chopped

Heat the oil in a large saucepan and throw in the lamb, a bit at a time, so that it seals and browns. Pour in the stock – enough to cover the meat – and bring to the boil. Reduce the heat to simmering point.

Make a bouquet garni of the chopped onion, coriander seeds and root ginger. To do this, put the ingredients on to a square of clean muslin, knot together the opposite ends to make a bundle and pop it in with the lamb. Simmer together everything for about 1 hour, then fish out the bundle and chuck it away. Make sure the lamb is tender – if it isn't, cook it for another 15 minutes or so.

Make a *picada* – a mixture of ingredients for thickening – from the almonds, cinnamon and some pepper. Stir this into the lamb, add some salt to taste, then stir in the hard-boiled eggs. Make sure it is all piping hot, then dish up, with some boiled rice as an accompaniment.

Castilian Roast Lamb

Cordero Asado a la Castellana

CENTRE-SPREAD PHOTOGRAPH BETWEEN PAGES 136 AND 137

When you order roast lamb in Spain you are invariably given a whole shoulder or leg from a very young animal. This has been simply seasoned with salt, pepper and garlic, probably placed on a bed of thickly-sliced potatoes, onions and whole garlic cloves, liberally soused in olive oil, put in a fiercely hot oven and roasted until the meat begins to fall off the bone and the onions and potatoes cook into a golden crunchy-topped pancake.

You could certainly add thickly-sliced potatoes and onions and garlic to the roasting tray while you prepare this wonderful aromatic dish.

Serves 4–6

1 × 1.5kg (3½lb) leg of lamb
2 tablespoons olive oil
Salt
Freshly ground black pepper
1 teaspoon paprika
1 teaspoon chopped fresh parsley
1 teaspoon chopped fresh oregano
1 teaspoon fresh thyme
2 cloves of garlic, sliced into thin slivers
1 wineglass dry white wine
300ml (½ pint) water
2 tablespoons wine vinegar
Juice of 1 lemon

Rub the lamb all over with half of the oil, then season it with salt and pepper. Mix together the paprika, parsley, oregano and thyme and rub this mixture over the surface of the lamb. Let the lamb sit for an hour so that these flavours can be absorbed.

Make some small slits in the leg of lamb and pop some slivers of garlic into them, then rub the lamb with the rest of the oil.

Sit the lamb in a roasting tin and put into a preheated oven, 230°C/450°F (gas mark 8), for 15 minutes. Meanwhile, put the white

wine, water, vinegar and lemon juice into a pan and bring to the boil.

Reduce the oven temperature to 190°C/375°F (gas mark 5). Pour about half the liquid over the meat and roast until it is done, basting from time to time with the liquid you have left. The length of cooking time depends on the size of your piece of lamb and how you like it cooked. Allow 15 minutes per 450g (1lb) if you like your lamb pink, 25 minutes per 450g (1lb) if you want it well done. The Spanish like their meats well done, but that doesn't mean you have to.

Slice and serve with gravy made from the herby-flavoured pan juices, roast potatoes and baby onions and Spinach or Chard with Raisins and Pine Nuts (see page 148).

Lamb with Red Peppers

Cordero con Pimientos Morrones

Serves 4

900g (2lb) boned leg of lamb, cut into cubes
Salt
Freshly ground black pepper
4 red peppers
4 tablespoons olive oil
3 cloves of garlic, finely sliced
1 large onion, chopped
200g (7oz) serrano *ham, finely diced*
5 large tomatoes, skinned and chopped (or use 1 × 397g [14oz] can tomatoes, drained, instead)
1 tablespoon paprika
1 wineglass cold water
1 wineglass dry white wine

Season the lamb with some salt and black pepper. Prepare the red peppers by roasting them in a preheated oven, 200°C/400°F (gas mark 6), for about 5 minutes, or by grilling them, turning frequently, until the outsides are blackened. Remove them from the oven (or grill) and pop a clean tea towel over them to trap the steam, then leave them to cool. (This makes them easier to peel.) Then peel and deseed them and slice into broad strips.

Heat the oil in a large flameproof casserole dish. Add the lamb, a handful at a time, and brown it over a fairly high heat. Add the garlic, onion and ham, and sauté for a few minutes, then throw in the peppers and tomatoes. Sprinkle in the paprika, stir it well, then pour in the water and the wine. Pop on the lid and cook for about 1½ hours, when the lamb should be tender and delicious. Serve with boiled potatoes.

Pork in Walnut Sauce

Cerdo en Nogada

Serves 4

900g (2lb) boneless loin of pork, as lean as possible, rolled and tied
Sea salt
50g (2oz) butter
Freshly grated nutmeg
Freshly ground black pepper
1 tablespoon brandy
600ml (1 pint) milk
100g (4oz) walnuts, shelled
4 small cooking apples, cored
25g (1oz) cornflour

Sprinkle the pork joint generously with the sea salt and leave it for an hour or so.

Rub half the butter over the pork and grate some nutmeg and pepper over it. (You could use ready-ground nutmeg at a pinch, but it doesn't taste a tenth as good. Invest in a nutmeg grater.)

Heat a deep flameproof casserole and pop in the pork joint; brown it well on all sides. Spoon in the brandy and set a match to it to flame the meat.

Transfer the pork to a roasting tin, pour over the milk and roast in a preheated oven, 200°C/400°F (gas mark 6), for 30 minutes. Then add the walnuts and cook for about another hour, until the meat is tender. Score the apples round their middles with a sharp knife and bake in the oven for the last 30 minutes or so on a separate dish with a knob of the remaining butter on each.

Lift out the pork. Thicken the pan juices with the cornflour, mixed with a little cold water, then strain the sauce into a jug. Carve the meat and serve it with the apples and some mashed potatoes. Hand round the sauce separately.

St Antonio's Stew

Olla de San Antón

In the days of old when food was scarce and meat was hard to come by, people would use any excuse to justify a celebration, however humble. And in the little village of Dúrcal near Granada, the following dish, probably cooked hundreds of years ago for the community by the baker, was dedicated to the local saint, name of Antón.

Seriously though, it is another of those rich, warming stews that demonstrates the influence of the new vegetables available after the discovery of America. Traditionally, because this is a party dish for ten or twelve people, they would add a pig's head split into two, with its ears. The pig's head would be cut into slices and served with all the rest, including the ears. More importantly, the pig's head would really enrich the stock. So if you add a skinned and singed pig's head to the ingredients, it will taste absolutely delicious.

Serves 4–6

225g (8oz) haricot beans, soaked overnight, then drained
4 tablespoons olive oil
450g (1lb) belly pork, cut into cubes
2 onions, chopped
2 cloves of garlic, crushed
1 wineglass dry white or rosé wine
1 ham bone
225g (8oz) potatoes, peeled and cut into chunks
100g (4oz) long-grain rice
175g (6oz) fennel, chopped
Salt
Freshly ground black pepper

First, blanch the soaked beans in boiling water for 15 minutes. Strain, rinse and strain again. Put to one side.

Meanwhile, heat the oil in a large saucepan and chuck in the pork, sizzling it well. Add the onions and garlic and fry them all together until they are golden, about 10 minutes. Add the wine and bubble it until it has reduced down – it won't take more than a few minutes.

Some happy holiday snaps!

One of me at the Alhambra

Another empty net......

Posing for Kim Sayer

Me and Miguel
after the sangria sketch!

Almond
Soup in the sky - Mallorca

Tim White demanding silence

Not the bayou –

just eel fishing.

The crew of la Refectorium Malaga – great lamb chops.

David Pritchard before he lost the hat – again.

If only James Burke
was here
Alhambra - Granada.

Resting
between
shots -
honest.

Take me back to the Black Hills -

with Dallas Love

Fill the pot with cold water and add the ham bone. Bring to the boil, add the beans, then cover and cook slowly for about 1¼ hours until the beans are beginning to soften.

Then add the potatoes, rice and fennel, continuing to cook for at least another half an hour to make sure everything is tender. Remove the ham bone and check the seasoning. This stew is in no rush to be eaten – it benefits from long, slow cooking.

José Luis' Sausage and Bean Dish

Butifarra con Alubias

This recipe was given to me by my particular chum, José Luis Izuel, who is a bit of a food historian and pointed out that haricot beans were brought over to Spain after the discovery of America. *Butifarra* is a white sausage from Catalonia that is spiced with cloves, nutmeg and cinnamon. If you cannot find it here, use Italian sweet sausage instead.

Serves 4–6

25g (1oz) lard
4 rashers streaky bacon, chopped
450g (1lb) butifarra *or Italian sweet sausage, sliced or left whole*
225g (8oz) haricot beans, soaked overnight, then cooked for about 1½ hours, until tender (or use 450g [1lb] canned beans)
Salt
Freshly ground black pepper
2 tablespoons chopped fresh parsley
Slivers of raw garlic

Heat the lard in a frying pan and fry the bacon until crisp. Remove it from the pan with a draining spoon and pop it on to kitchen paper.

Put the sausage into the pan and cook for about 5–8 minutes, depending on whether you sliced it or left it whole, then remove and put with the bacon.

Add the haricot beans to the pan and cook for about 3 or 4 minutes to heat them through, then return the bacon and sausage back to the pan, stirring well to reheat for a couple of minutes. Season and dish up, sprinkled with a mix of finely chopped parsley and garlic.

Roast Suckling Pig

Lechón Asado

The way the Spanish serve suckling pig is not for the squeamish and faint-hearted because they do have a liking for very, very small suckling pigs probably weighing only 2kg (4lb) or so.

But, believe me, one of those split in half and rubbed with salt and sprinkled with thyme and rosemary and roasted in a fiercely hot oven is a real treat. You just don't want to look at it too closely, that's all. It makes great finger food if you chop it up after cooking.

Serves 6–8, but cook 2 or 3 for a party

1 suckling pig, weighing about 3kg (6½lb)
100g (4oz) lard
4 cloves of garlic, crushed
4 bay leaves
4 sprigs of fresh thyme
4 sprigs of fresh rosemary
2 tablespoons salt
Freshly ground black pepper
2–3 tablespoons dry white wine
1 tablespoon lemon juice
1 tablespoon cold water

First of all you have to split the suckling pig in half lengthways down the underside, keeping the head intact. Then you have to pound it down a bit, so that it splays open. You could save yourself the aggravation and ask your butcher to do the necessaries for you.

Melt the lard in a small saucepan, and add the crushed garlic. Use a brush to paint this all over the pig, saving half for later.

Put the bay leaves, thyme and half the rosemary in a big roasting dish – the Spaniards tend to use earthenware ones, as they reckon this gives their roasts a better flavour and they're probably right. Anyway, lift the pig on top, skin side down, and season with 1 tablespoon of the salt, a few good twists of freshly ground black pepper and the rest of the rosemary. Add the wine to the dish and pop it into a preheated oven, 220°C/425°F (gas mark 7), for 10 minutes. Reduce the heat to

180°C/350°F (gas mark 4) and continue to cook for another hour. Remove the pig from the oven and turn it over, covering the ears and tail with some foil to prevent them from burning.

Stab the skin with a fork here and there and brush over the remaining lard and garlic mixture. Mix together the rest of the salt with the lemon juice and water and brush this over the skin. Return the pig to the oven, where it will need another 1¼ hours or so. Baste it occasionally with any remaining lemon juice and water to crisp the skin.

Tastes particularly good with some of my delicious Aubergine Purée (see page 151).

Empanada

PHOTOGRAPH OPPOSITE PAGE 104

It struck me that *empanada* is to the Galicians what the pasty is to the Cornish – only flatter: a thin sandwich of shortcrust pastry stuffed with savoury goodies. Like a pasty, *empanada* can be very good – or revoltingly bad.

I only say this because the first time I tasted *empanada* Pritchard had ordered us all out of bed at the crack of dawn, to look for a location to film the Floyd pilgrim bit – you know, walking towards Santiago de Compostela, complete with staff, scallop shell emblem and pilgrim's picnic of *empanada*. But after a futile search Pritchard's stomach, as usual, got the better of him, he declared the mission unaccomplished and we broke for our picnic lunch. We did better the next day at Monte Pedroso, among the eucalyptus and pine trees. But even then there were complications. Steve, our trusty lighting man, who often had to double up as driver, reversed our van into a hidden pit – which we called the Pilgrim's Trap.

Anyway, there are lots of different recipes for *empanada*, which can be sweet or savoury or both. In former times working men would carry it to their mines, factories or fields. Nowadays it is baked in fabulous rectangular or circular shapes, cut into bite-sized pieces and offered as one of the most delicious *tapas* to be found in the whole of Spain.

Serves 6

For the yeast dough

15g (½oz) fresh yeast, or 1½ teaspoons dried yeast plus
1 teaspoon caster sugar
4 tablespoons warm water
450g (1lb) strong plain flour
1 teaspoon salt
3 tablespoons lard, melted
2 eggs, lightly beaten
120ml (4fl oz) warm milk

For the filling

325g (12oz) pork fillet, thinly sliced
1 teaspoon paprika
2 cloves of garlic, finely chopped
1 teaspoon fresh chopped oregano
Salt
Freshly ground black pepper
4 tablespoons olive oil
2 small onions, chopped
1 large green pepper, cored, seeded and sliced into strips
3 tomatoes, skinned and chopped
1 tablespoon fresh chopped parsley
2 hard-boiled eggs, shelled and sliced
2 small red pimientos (canned), drained and sliced
1 egg, beaten

To make the dough, mix the fresh or dried yeast with the warm water, adding 1 teaspoon of sugar if using dried yeast. Put the flour and salt into a large bowl and add the cooled, melted lard and the lightly beaten eggs. Pour in the yeast mixture and the warm milk and mix well with your fingers to combine all the ingredients.

Turn the dough out on to a lightly floured surface and knead it for a good 5 minutes to give a smooth and elastic dough. Now pop it into a lightly oiled bowl and leave to rise for about $1^1/_2$ hours, covered with a clean tea-towel. Knock the dough back and knead for another 2 or 3 minutes – lightly this time – then leave it to rise again for a further hour in the same bowl.

While the dough is rising for the second time, start to prepare the filling. Sprinkle the sliced pork with paprika, 1 clove of chopped garlic and the oregano. Season with some salt and pepper and leave for 30 minutes.

Heat the oil in a frying pan and quickly fry the pork slices over a high heat, then remove them. Add the onions, pepper and remaining garlic to the pan, stirring well for a minute or two. Then stir in the tomatoes and parsley and simmer gently until the tomatoes are reduced and the sauce is thickened. Cool slightly.

Divide the *empanada* dough in two and roll out one half to a thickness of around 2cm ($^3/_4$ inch). Line a large cake tin or small roasting pan with this dough and pour over half the sauce. Arrange the pork slices on top, with the hard-boiled eggs and pimientos, then cover with the remaining sauce.

Use the remaining dough to cover the pie (roll it out first!). Dampen the edges to seal them, then decorate the pie as you fancy, making sure you leave a small vent for the steam to escape.

Bake in a medium oven, 180°C/350°F (gas mark 4), for 30 minutes. Remove from the oven so that you can brush the top of the pie with beaten egg, then return it to brown nicely for another 15 minutes.

Pork Chops, Madrid-Style

Chuletas de Cerdo a la Madrileña

CENTRE-SPREAD PHOTOGRAPH BETWEEN PAGES 136 AND 137

The Spanish so enjoy fat, milk-fed pork that even the simplest chop thrown on to a barbecue anywhere in Spain seems to taste much better than our rubber-fleshed English chops. Perhaps it is because they always buy their pork fresh rather than frozen. If you can buy milk-fed, white-fleshed chops this dish will be much enhanced.

Serves 4

4 pork chops, rind removed if you prefer
2 tablespoons olive oil (optional)

For the marinade
3 tablespoons olive oil
3 cloves of garlic, finely chopped
1 bay leaf, torn into pieces
1 teaspoon paprika
1 tablespoon chopped fresh parsley
Salt
Freshly ground black pepper

Mix together all the ingredients for the marinade in a shallow dish (not aluminium), large enough to lay the pork chops in. Marinate the chops for at least 1½ hours or longer, and do not forget to turn them over from time to time.

To cook the chops, you can either bake them in an oiled casserole dish in a preheated oven, 180°C/350°F (gas mark 4), for about 25–30 minutes, basting them frequently with the marinade. Alternatively, you can cook them on top of the stove. Heat 2 tablespoons of oil in a large frying pan. Fry the chops briskly for 2 or 3 minutes, turning once, then add the marinade. Reduce the heat and cook gently for about 10 minutes on each side, until the chops are tender.

Delicious served with fried potatoes and a fresh salad or green vegetables.

Pork and Cabbage Stew

Patachú

In the rare moments of sanity when I escape to Ireland I look forward with tummy-rumbling anticipation to a plate of boiled bacon and cabbage, a classic Irish dish. When I visit Alsace or Germany the thought of smoked knuckle of pig pressed with pickled cabbage is equally pleasant. When I go to my favourite Chinese restaurant in Bristol I invariably have pork and salted greens. What I am trying to say is, the combination of pork and cabbage, be it bacon or Chinese roast loin, is high on my list of favourites. And when my chum Francine, of La Dida Restaurante in Barcelona, showed me this recipe I was delighted.

Serves 4–6

225g (8oz) haricot beans, soaked overnight
(or use 450g [1lb] canned white beans)
6 tablespoons olive oil
2 large onions, chopped
2 cloves of garlic, crushed
225g (8oz) pork spare ribs
4 large potatoes, peeled and cut into chunks
4 courgettes, sliced
1 big green crunchy cabbage, with a firm white heart, shredded
Salt
Freshly ground black pepper
1 tomato, skinned and chopped

Boil the beans in plenty of lightly salted water for 15 minutes, then reduce the heat and cook for about 1¼ hours, until they are tender. (No need, of course, to do this if you use canned beans.)

Pour the oil into a large saucepan and heat it up. Tip in the onions, garlic and pork ribs and fry them gently for about 20 minutes, until golden. Add plenty of water, about 2 litres (4½ pints), and bring to the boil. Simmer for about 15 minutes, then add the potatoes. Cook for another 20 minutes or so until the ribs are done – taste them to check – and the potatoes are tender. Add the courgettes and cabbage and cook for a few minutes, then add the cooked beans. Heat through, season and serve, sprinkled with the chopped tomato.

Sausages with Sweet and Sour Figs

Salchicha con Higos

Serves 4

For the sweet and sour figs
250ml (8fl oz) red wine vinegar
100g (4oz) sugar
3 whole cloves
1 × 5cm (2 inch) piece of cinnamon stick
1 lemon wedge
1 orange wedge
450g (1lb) fresh green figs

675g (1½lb) spicy sausages
1 tablespoon olive oil
4 tablespoons dry white wine
4 tablespoons cold water
1 tablespoon tomato sauce (see page 13) or use tomato purée
Salt
Freshly ground black pepper

To make the sweet and sour figs, put all the ingredients for them, except the figs, into a saucepan. Bring them up to boiling point, reduce the heat and bubble for 5 minutes. Next, add the figs and simmer for 15 minutes. (You can use bottled figs, in which case you just need to cook them for 5 minutes.) Remove from the heat and let the figs sit in this syrup overnight, covered with a lid, or clingfilm.

Next day, cook the sausages by frying them in the oil for a few minutes to brown a little, then add half the wine. When the sausages are cooked and brown and the liquid has all but evaporated – about 15–20 minutes – transfer them to a warm platter. Discard most of the fat from the pan.

Pour the remaining wine and water into the pan, add the tomato sauce or purée, then season with some salt and pepper. Simmer for a couple of minutes to bring the flavours together, then pop the sausages back into the pan. Drain the figs and add them too. Heat gently for a couple of minutes to make sure that everything is piping hot. Serve with potatoes.

Spicy Spanish Sausage

Chorizo

Happily, you can buy these coarse-textured Spanish sausages, which are flavoured with paprika and garlic, at many good delicatessens. But if you fancy yourself as a sausage-maker, I have included this recipe.

Makes approximately 775g (1¾lb)

450g (1lb) lean pork loin, chopped into small cubes
275g (10oz) pork fat, chopped into small cubes
2½ teaspoons coarse salt
½ teaspoon freshly ground black pepper
2½ tablespoons paprika
½ teaspoon ground cumin
½ teaspoon ground coriander
½ teaspoon caster sugar
4 tablespoons dry red wine
2 cloves of garlic, very finely chopped
1½ teaspoons crushed dried red chilli pepper
¾ teaspoon saltpetre (to preserve them)
Sausage casings, for stuffing (ask your butcher)

Find a large bowl and chuck everything into it, apart from the sausage casings. Mix it all together until thoroughly combined, then cover the bowl and chill for several hours – overnight, if you like.

You can either pipe the sausagemeat into the casings using a piping bag, fitted with a large, plain nozzle, pushing the mixture down the casings as you go. Alternatively, you can use a sausage stuffing attachment fitted to your food processor, if you have one. Twist and tie the sausages every so often – at sausage-length intervals.

Hang up the sausage links to dry for 2–3 days, well away from any comic book dogs, who may wish to run off with them. Then put them into the refrigerator and cover with waxed paper (greaseproof will do). They will be ready to use in a few days, but will keep for several weeks. You can either grill them on the barbecue or fry them in a pan, or use in stews.

Grilled Pig's Trotters

Manitas de Cerdo a la Parrilla

Serves 6

6 pig's trotters, split lengthways and washed well
1 large carrot, roughly chopped
1 large onion, peeled and quartered
2 bay leaves
6 black peppercorns, crushed
2 wineglasses dry sherry
Salt

For grilling

4 tablespoons fresh breadcrumbs – white or brown as you wish
3 tablespoons chopped fresh parsley
2 cloves of garlic, finely chopped
Salt
Freshly ground black pepper
3 tablespoons olive oil

Put the pig's trotters in pairs in a very large saucepan, so that they make a nice tight fit. Throw in the carrot, onion, bay leaves and peppercorns. Pour in the sherry and enough water to cover well, then add a little salt. Boil steadily for 40 minutes.

Top up the pan with some more boiling water, then lower the heat and simmer gently with the lid on for about 4 hours. It will take this long for the trotters to become really tender, and by this time they will be falling to bits. You could make some splints from thin sheets of wood, from a vegetable box, for example, and wrap them round with muslin so that the trotters keep their shape while cooking. Don't forget to check the pan from time to time to make sure that it is not going to boil dry – keep topping up with more boiling water as it is needed.

When the 4 hours are up, turn off the heat and let the trotters cool down in the liquid. Remove and drain them, then put into a shallow ovenproof casserole dish. Pop them into a preheated oven, 200°C/400°F (gas mark 6), for about 15 minutes to reheat. Sprinkle them with the breadcrumbs, parsley, garlic, salt and pepper. Drizzle over the oil and whack under a preheated hot grill until nicely crisp.

Serve with a crisp watercress salad and some spiced oranges.

Veal with Mushrooms

Ternera con Setas

CENTRE-SPREAD PHOTOGRAPH BETWEEN PAGES 136 AND 137

Serves 4

675g (1½lb) stewing veal, cut into chunks
25g (1oz) cornflour
Salt
Freshly ground black pepper
6 tablespoons olive oil
1 onion, chopped
225g (8oz) tomatoes, skinned and chopped
1 wineglass medium dry white wine or sweet sherry
250ml (8fl oz) veal or chicken stock
450g (1lb) field mushrooms, roughly chopped

Roll the meat in the cornflour, which you have seasoned with some salt and pepper. Heat the oil in a large frying pan and add the meat, a handful at a time, so that it browns. Lift it out with a draining spoon and pop it into a flameproof casserole.

In the same oil sauté the onion for about 3–4 minutes, until it is transparent. Tip in the tomatoes and wine (or sherry), then a splash of stock and a dash more salt and pepper. Let it boil for 5 minutes so that some of the liquid evaporates.

Pour this lot over the meat in the casserole, bring up to boiling point again and allow to simmer – either on the hob or in a fairly hot oven, 190°C/375°F (gas mark 5) – for about 30 minutes, or until the meat is nearly tender. Add the mushrooms, some more stock as needed, and leave it to cook until the meat is really tender – another 15 minutes or so should do the trick.

Veal Manchega

Ternera Manchego

In Spain veal or young beef seems to be much more common than what I call proper English beef. Personally, I find the beef sometimes a little bland, but made with a bit of decent veal this dish is really quite good. Again, it is a pretty healthy one because veal doesn't have any fat and olive oil is good for you.

Serves 6

900g (2lb) veal fillet, cut lengthways into six strips
Salt
6 tablespoons lemon juice
2 small onions, chopped
3 medium red peppers, cored, seeded and chopped
3 medium tomatoes, skinned and chopped
150ml (1/4 pint) olive oil

Rinse the veal and pat it dry with kitchen paper, then put it into a large, shallow casserole dish in a single layer. Season it with a good sprinkling of salt and the lemon juice.

Strew the chopped onions, peppers and tomatoes over the top and pour over the oil. Now pop on the lid and simmer gently on top of the stove for about 1 hour, until the veal is tender. If you like, you can put the casserole in a preheated oven, 190°C/375°F (gas mark 5), for about the same amount of time.

Eat it with some fried potatoes or just some hunks of crusty bread to mop up the juices.

Lamb's Fry

Frituras Mallorquinas

When you visit a new restaurant it is always a good idea to position yourself carefully so that as you sip your apéritif you can watch the waiters taking trays of food to the regulars. I was doing this on the terrace of a small restaurant in Majorca and the man next to me – I wasn't staring, honest – was eating what looked like Chinese stir-fried mixed meats and peppers. It was a colourful dish and had arrived sizzling, so I ordered some for myself and discovered *Frituras Mallorquinas*.

Lovers of offal will enjoy this dish. Basically, it is little pieces of heart, liver and sweetbreads fried with peppers, paprika and potatoes. I enthused mightily about it to my director, David Pritchard, who said, 'It sounds like a perfect one for an outdoor cooking sketch.'

So we hurtled round the island looking for the right location and, of course, knowing I can't stand heights, he chose a precipitous cliff edge, which I swear was several thousand feet above the sea. It was late in the afternoon when we finally set up: Clive wanted me silhouetted against the sky standing right on the edge, which I refused to do and tempers were becoming a little frayed. I was genuinely nervous for it makes me physically ill to stand next to a long drop.

Anyhow, after several false starts filming got under way, and it was then I realised I had forgotten to bring the potatoes which, cut into batons, are such an important part of this dish.

It was out of the question to return the 30 or 40 miles to Palma as time was pressing, but an eagle-eyed crew member spotted what looked like a tiny village by the ocean below us. It took nearly an hour to reach, along a tortuous, hairpinned, potholed track that was roughly hewn out of the side of the mountain. There were no safety barriers; it was a petrifying drive.

When we reached what we thought was the village we found a sort of abandoned housing estate. Obviously, the grand dream of a holiday complex on the Mediterranean had run short of funds. Only a few of the houses had been completed and there was an overall air of desolation. But there was a small bar, which we entered.

As we walked in, probably looking extremely silly in our shorts and T-shirts, the room fell silent. Eventually, David Pritchard plucked up courage and in an embarrassing combination of Spanish, English, Englishman-abroad-speak and gestures, one of which was pointing his left arm directly out at an angle from his body and making a winding motion with his right, 'Me, Television Englishe from the BBC, old chap' – he then pointed to the ceiling. I knew what he meant – that we were stranded on top of the mountain. All this was completely incomprehensible to the astounded patrons of the bar and I was now in hysterics and unable to help in any way. Our needs were limited, but we needed a fairly plausible story to ask a barman for just three potatoes.

Anyway, after three or four beers and more garbled conversation we managed to acquire the spuds and set off back to the mountain top, in time to film against the setting sun and just as the mosquitos were really beginning to bite.

Serves 4

1 whole lamb's fry – liver, heart, lights (lungs and sweetbreads)
8 tablespoons olive oil
2 onions, roughly chopped
5 cloves of garlic, chopped
3 green peppers, cored, seeded and roughly chopped
2 tablespoons paprika
1½ wineglasses dry white wine
1 wineglass cold water
450g (1lb) potatoes, cut into chunks or batons
Salt
Freshly ground black pepper

First, prepare the lamb's fry. You will have to trim the liver, snipping away any connective tissue and removing the membrane. Trim away any fat surrounding the heart, then cut out the arteries and fibrous tissue. Do likewise with the lungs. Ideally, the sweetbreads need to be soaked for a couple of hours to clean them. Snip away any discoloured parts, then blanch by popping them in cold water, bringing them up to the boil and simmering for 3–4 minutes. Drain and then trim them, pulling away the ducts and removing the outer pieces of membrane. Now slice the lot.

Heat 3 tablespoons of oil in a large frying pan and add the lungs, sautéeing gently for 5 minutes. Add the rest of the sliced offal and fry gently for about 20 minutes, until tender. Remove and keep warm.

Meanwhile, in a separate pan, heat 2 tablespoons of oil and fry the onions, garlic and peppers for a few minutes, then stir in the paprika. Add the wine and water and bring up to bubbling point. Turn down the heat and cook until the vegetables are tender and the sauce has reduced – about 15 minutes.

Wipe out the first pan and add the rest of the oil. Heat it up and tip in the potatoes, frying them gently until they are tender and golden brown, stirring every now and then. This will take 15–20 minutes.

Now mix together all the ingredients. Season with salt and pepper and heat through for about 5 minutes.

Tongue with a Pomegranate Sauce

Langua en Salsa de Granada

Serves 4

4 pork tongues, rinsed and soaked in salted water for 2 hours, then drained
50g (2oz) lard
1 onion, chopped
2 pomegranates, quartered and seeds extracted
250ml (8fl oz) meat stock
90ml (3fl oz) dry sherry
Salt
Freshly ground black pepper

Put the soaked tongues in a large pan, covering them with some fresh water. Bring up to the boil, then reduce the heat and simmer gently, with the lid on, for about half an hour. Drain away the cooking water and let the tongues cool down enough so that you can remove the skin.

Heat the lard in a large saucepan or flameproof casserole. Throw in the onion and fry it for a couple of minutes, then add the tongues and sauté them together until they have browned. Add the pomegranate seeds, stock, sherry and seasonings and simmer for about 1 hour. The tongues should be tender, and you should slice them before serving.

A surprising little number, as it's not every day that you eat tongue or pomegranates – let alone together.

Tripe, Madrid-Style

Callos a la Madrileña

Serves 4

450g (1lb) tripe
4 tablespoons olive oil
2 onions, chopped
3 cloves of garlic, finely chopped
1 tablespoon paprika
100g (4oz) piece of Spanish salami or chorizo, *diced*
2 wineglasses dry white wine
4 tomatoes, skinned and chopped
2 teaspoons fresh thyme
2 fresh or dried chilli peppers, seeded and chopped
2 bay leaves
6 peppercorns, crushed
Salt
175g (6oz) cooked chick peas, drained
3 tablespoons chopped fresh parsley

Tripe is sold parboiled, but when you get it home you should soak it for 5 minutes or so in cold water, then rinse thoroughly and drain well. Cut it up into 5cm (2 inch) squares. How long you cook it depends on how tender the tripe is – it will need between one and two hours.

In a large flameproof casserole dish, or a large frying pan, heat the oil and sauté the onions and garlic for about 5 minutes, until softly golden. Stir in the paprika, tripe and salami or *chorizo*, then add the wine and bubble it up. Chuck in the tomatoes, thyme, chilli, bay leaves and peppercorns, and season with some salt. Cook over a low heat until the tripe is tender (as I said, between one and two hours but taste it after 1 hour to see how it is doing). By this time you will have a deliciously rich, thick sauce. Fish out and throw away the bay leaves, then add the chick peas and stir them through. Heat for 3–4 minutes, then serve, sprinkled liberally with the parsley.

Opposite: Gypsy Stew (page 142)
Next page, from left to right: Veal with Mushrooms (page 131); Pork Chops, Madrid-Style (page 126); Castilian Roast Lamb (page 116)

Oxtail Stew

Guiso de Rabo de Toro

PHOTOGRAPH OPPOSITE PAGE 105

There is a delightful restaurant perched on the side of a hill in the tiny village of San Prudencio in the Basque Country, where we stopped for Sunday lunch. I had a great plate of oxtail, but for me it was a little spoilt because they had added a bit of Pernod, Pastis or anis. Unless you are passionately fond of anis I wouldn't put any in.

Serves 4–6

2kg (4½lb) oxtail, chopped into pieces
(don't forget to remove excessive fat)
2 tablespoons plain flour
Salt
Freshly ground black pepper
50g (2oz) lard
2 tablespoons olive oil
2 medium onions, chopped
2 cloves of garlic, chopped
2 large carrots, sliced
2 sticks of celery, chopped
2 bay leaves
2 sprigs of fresh parsley
1 sprig of fresh thyme
1 teaspoon paprika
250ml (8fl oz) dry white wine
600ml (1 pint) beef stock
A dash of Pernod or anis (optional)

Coat the pieces of oxtail with flour seasoned with the salt and pepper. Heat the lard in a very large pan and brown the oxtail well – this is what will give your stew a great flavour. Transfer the oxtail to a large, flameproof casserole and discard the lard.

Top Spinach with Raisins and Pine Nuts (page 148); ***Centre*** Poor Man's Potatoes (page 153); ***Bottom*** Broad Beans with Black Pudding (page 145)

Spoon the oil into the pan you've just emptied and brown the onions and garlic, then tip these into the casserole with the oxtail. Add all the other ingredients – the liquid should just cover the oxtail and vegetables. If not, add a little extra water.

Bring up to bubbling point, then reduce the heat and cook gently for 3–3½ hours, until the oxtail is really tender – it needs to be falling off the bone.

Remove the oxtail with a slotted spoon and keep warm. Skim the fat from the surface of the sauce, then bubble the sauce to reduce it a little. Check the seasoning, then pop the meat back and reheat it. Remove the bay leaves before serving. The Spanish often add a little anis to the sauce – but I don't care for it.

Terrific with green beans, and boiled or mashed potatoes. A dry red Riojan wine goes well with this.

VEGETABLES AND SALADS

Artichokes Braised in Wine

Alcachofas Cocidas en Vino

Serves 4

6 artichokes, washed (choose small ones)
Juice of ½ lemon
4 tablespoons olive oil
1 small onion, finely chopped
2 cloves of garlic, finely sliced
250ml (8fl oz) dry white wine
Salt
Freshly grated nutmeg

Chop off the stalks from the artichokes and strip off their tough outer leaves. Now quarter them, and if there is some hairy choke to be removed do it with a small, sharp knife. Drop the pieces of artichoke into a large bowl of water to which you have added the lemon juice. Do this as you go along to stop any discoloration. When you've prepared all of them, you can pour away the water and drain the artichokes well. Turn to page 203 for fuller notes on preparing artichokes.

Heat the oil in a large frying pan or flameproof casserole. Pop in the onion and garlic and sauté gently for about 5 minutes. Throw in the artichokes and fry for a minute or two, then pour in the wine. Add a shake of salt and enough water almost to cover the artichokes. Put on the lid and simmer for 10 minutes, then remove it and bubble away for about 30 minutes more, until the artichokes are cooked – their leaves can be pulled off easily when they are done.

A Bread and Vegetable Hotpot

Sopa Mallorquina

For those of you whose Spanish is as bad as mine, at first glance you might think that this is a soup recipe. Absolutely not so. It is a sturdy vegetable stew much beloved of the Majorcan people. Even though it has no meat its happy mix of vegetable flavours and bread will appeal to the heartiest of trenchermen on a cold winter's day.

Serves 8 or more

2 large onions, chopped
300ml (½ pint) olive oil
6 leeks, trimmed and sliced
6 spring onions, trimmed and chopped
3 red peppers, cored, seeded and chopped
3 green peppers, cored, seeded and chopped
5–6 medium potatoes, peeled and sliced
1 bulb of garlic – crush the cloves but do not peel them
1 small cauliflower, broken into florets
100g (4oz) peas or cooked haricot beans
2 hearts of white cabbage, chopped
4 large, very ripe tomatoes, chopped
2 bay leaves
A handful of chopped fresh parsley
2–3 dried red chilli peppers
Salt
Freshly ground black pepper
1 loaf of nutty brown bread –
the type you buy from health food stores, sliced

First, fry the onions in about 3 tablespoons of the oil, which you have heated up in a frying pan. When they are golden and soft, transfer them to an extremely large lidded saucepan. Work your way down the list of ingredients, adding them in the same order to the pot, until you get to the salt and pepper. Stir well, put on the lid and simmer very gently for a long time over a low heat – about 1 hour – until the flavours are blended. Transfer about half of this mixture to an earthenware dish, if you want to be authentically Spanish, otherwise to whatever suitable vessel you possess. Fish out and discard the bay leaves. Put a layer of sliced bread on top, pour over the oil you have left, cover with the rest of the vegetables and bake in a preheated hot oven, 200°C/400°F (gas mark 6), for about 15 minutes.

Vegetable Hotpot

Potaje

Serves lots

225g (8oz) white haricot beans, soaked overnight, then drained
1 piece of ham on the bone, weighing about 900g (2lb)
1 onion, chopped
1 leek, trimmed and sliced
2–3 cloves of garlic, crushed
2 tomatoes, skinned and chopped
225g (8oz) runner beans, sliced
1 large carrot, sliced
3 medium potatoes, peeled and cut into chunks
100g (4oz) cauliflower, broken into florets
Handful of chard, chopped
1 bay leaf
Salt
Freshly ground black pepper

Put the soaked beans into a very large saucepan with the ham bone. Cover with water and bring to the boil. Keep boiling for 15 minutes – this is necessary for the beans – then turn the heat down low and cook slowly, covered, for about 1 hour. Skim the surface, throw in the onion, leek and garlic and continue cooking for another 30 minutes.

Now add the tomatoes, runner beans, carrot, potatoes, cauliflower and chard. Pop in the bay leaf and simmer until all the vegetables are cooked and the beans are tender. This will take another 20–30 minutes.

Take out the ham bone and scrape off the meat – it will just fall off. Return the meat to the pan and discard the bone. Taste the stew and add some pepper – it may need some salt, but it is unlikely. Serve in bowls with some crusty bread. This dish can be reheated.

Gypsy Stew

Olla Gitana

PHOTOGRAPH OPPOSITE PAGE 136

This is an old Moorish recipe that fascinated me; it is basically a stew of pumpkin, fruit, pulses and beans. A curious combination, but I decided to cook it because one of our crew was a committed vegetarian and agreed to be the guinea pig.

In fact, the end result was amazing; it was like a little spicy vegetable *thalie* I sometimes eat at my favourite Indian restaurant, except that it didn't have the strong Indian spices in it. But there would be nothing wrong with adding a bit of ginger and chilli to gee it up. A great dish.

Serves 8

450g (1lb) chick peas, soaked overnight, then drained
150ml (1/4 pint) olive oil
2 onions, chopped
2 ripe tomatoes, skinned and chopped
450g (1lb) green beans, sliced
275g (10oz) pumpkin, peeled and cut into chunks
Salt
Freshly ground black pepper
About 600ml (1 pint) vegetable stock
6 firm pears, peeled and chopped
2 slices of white bread
2 cloves of garlic, finely chopped
20 blanched almonds, toasted
4 tablespoons white wine vinegar
Few saffron strands
2 tablespoons paprika

Bring a very large pan of water – you'll need about 3 litres (7 pints) – to the boil. Add the chick peas and simmer for about 1 hour, until almost cooked. Strain and reserve.

While the chick peas are cooking, heat a couple of tablespoons of the oil in a saucepan and add the onions and tomatoes. Pop on the lid and turn down the heat, leaving them to sweat for about 30 minutes, stirring occasionally.

When the tomatoes and onions are really soft, add the chick peas along with the green beans and pumpkin. Season with salt and pepper. Cover with the stock and simmer gently for about 20 minutes, adding the pears about 8–10 minutes before the end of the cooking time.

Heat the rest of the oil in a small frying pan and fry the slices of bread with the garlic until golden. Remove from the pan and drain on kitchen paper. Reserve the oil.

Now make a *picada* – a paste for thickening and flavouring – from the almonds, fried bread, garlic, vinegar, reserved oil, saffron and paprika. Grind everything down using a pestle and mortar or be lazy and use a food processor or blender. Add a little of the liquid from the pan to make a smooth paste.

Add the *picada* to other ingredients in the pan, stirring well to thicken. Check the vegetables for tenderness and serve piping hot in soup bowls.

Mixed Vegetables, Spanish-Style

Menestra de Verduras

PHOTOGRAPH OPPOSITE PAGE 168

Mixed Vegetables, Spanish-Style, *Menestra de Verduras*, is found on every menu throughout Spain – as the name implies, a little stew of mixed vegetables. It can vary from a pre-prepared pack of frozen vegetables to a most scrumptious selection of fresh ones, delicately and lightly cooked. I found it a wonderful accompaniment to a sauceless dish of, say, pork chops or lamb cutlets or straightforward plain chicken. In Spain it is served in restaurants as a separate course and so makes a good starter too. You don't have to be hidebound by the vegetables I have specified here; you can mix and match as you wish.

Serves 4–6

Salt
4 carrots, diced
4 artichoke hearts, quartered
125g (5oz) green beans, sliced into 2.5cm (1 inch) pieces
125g (5oz) fresh broad beans, shelled
125g (5oz) fresh peas, shelled
4 tablespoons olive oil
1 small onion, chopped
1 clove of garlic, finely chopped
1 red pepper, cored, seeded and chopped
75g (3oz) serrano *ham, diced*
1 tablespoon plain flour
2 teaspoons paprika
3 tablespoons tomato purée
Freshly ground black pepper
Chopped fresh mint or parsley } *to garnish (optional)*
2 hard-boiled eggs, chopped }

In a large saucepan, bring some water to the boil to cook the vegetables – don't use gallons or else all the vitamins and flavour will leach out and will go down the drain with the water. Add a little salt to this water and cook the carrots for about 5 minutes, then add the artichoke hearts, followed by the green beans, the broad beans and, lastly, the peas and cook for a further 10 minutes or so, until the vegetables are tender. Do not overcook – remove the vegetables with a slotted spoon as they become just tender. Drain, reserving the water for stock, and keep warm.

Heat the oil in a large frying pan and fry the onion and garlic until softened, about 2–3 minutes. Add the red pepper and diced ham and cook gently for about 4 or 5 minutes.

Throw in the cooked, drained vegetables, stirring well to mix and reheat. Combine the flour with the paprika, tomato purée and about 125ml (4fl oz) reserved vegetable water and add this to the pot, stirring it well while the mixture thickens a little. Cook the lot together over a gentle heat for about 10 minutes, then taste and adjust the seasoning.

Dish out among your guests, garnishing, if you like, with mint or parsley and chopped hard-boiled egg.

Broad Beans with Black Pudding

Habas a la Catalana

PHOTOGRAPH OPPOSITE PAGE 137

Do you realise that if Christopher Columbus, or whoever it was who discovered America, hadn't, the Western world would have been deprived of one of the great culinary masterpieces of all times – Heinz baked beans. And without the beans that came from the New World nor would there be any *cassoulets, soupe au pistous* or *cocidas*, the stews, of Spanish cookery – in short, the world would be a worse place. There are plenty of other things from the New World that are absolutely abominable, but beans and baked beans are not one of them.

Broad beans, however, are a different matter. The Old World has always known these. When I was a kid my sister and I took great delight, after our parents had gone to bed, in creeping back downstairs and having midnight feasts. One of my specialities, usually on a Sunday night, was to raid the larder and find the cooked broad beans leftover from Sunday lunch. It was the 1950s and we didn't have rashers of bacon, we had bacon bits. And because these were cheap, mostly

fat with a little meat, I used to dice the bits even more and then fry them until they became crunchy little morselets. Then I would add the broad beans to the sizzling hot fat in the pan and cook them with the hot bacon for a minute before eating them with relish.

The broad bean in Spain, up to the late fifteenth century, was the staple diet of the rural Spanish and indeed even today the broad bean, fresh or dried, is held in high esteem. The broad bean, for me, is one of the best vegetables in the world, especially if you cook them slowly and peel off the pods before plunging them into fiercely boiling water.

Anyway, one day we were in Barcelona and the production manager, actually the production manageress, gave us the schedule for the following day that said, 'Drive a couple of hours to Bertren (sic), rendezvous there at the Hotel Tuca, and we will do our cooking sketch in the Pyrenees.'

Off we set and after five hours of driving we were becoming a little worried. We stopped to check the route again. These instructions were wrong, it was taking too long, we wouldn't be there till midnight at this rate. We looked at the schedule to verify it. We checked, double-checked and cross-checked to verify it. Contrary to instructions, we still had another hundred or so miles to go.

Then my assistant Anne said: 'Isn't that funny, here we are poring over the map and there is a sign that says Hotel Tuca. Isn't that odd! But hold on a minute, what is the name of this town? Ah well! It's called Betren.' Doubt and worry clouded us like an incoming fog.

'Isn't it odd there should be two names so far apart, so similar.'

'Let's go to this hotel anyway, just in case.'

Thank God we did, because the production manager had misspelt the name and it could have been a disaster, except for the brilliant inspiration of our supremely good selves. But to get back to the broad beans, which in honour of our production manager I will call 'broad beans à la Rubin' – no names, no pack drill, nudge nudge, wink wink.

If I may digress for another second – in our travels round the world every time we climb on to a boat for one of our fishing sequences, the captain never fails to tell me that this particular place experiences the highest rise and fall of the tide in the entire world. Similarly, in Spain, every restaurant is the one favoured by King Juan Carlos. 'This is *the* restaurant,' they whisper conspiratorially and proudly; 'this is the only one he goes to.'

Imagine my delight when having got over the grumpiness, we discovered that what was in season, to be found everywhere in overflowing baskets, was broad beans. Moreover, it seemed that one of the great delicacies of the area is only a slightly more complicated version, with black pudding, of my favourite childhood feast. I commend it to the house.

Serves 4

2 tablespoons olive oil
175g (6oz) belly pork, rinded and diced into 7mm (1/4 inch) cubes
4 rashers back bacon, rinded and chopped
175g (6oz) black pudding, sliced
450g (1lb) shelled broad beans (these would weigh about 1.4kg [3lb] in their pods)
1 tablespoon chopped fresh mint
1 teaspoon sugar
1 generous dash of dry white wine (about 1/2 a wineglass)
Salt, maybe
Freshly ground black pepper

Heat the oil in a large frying pan and pop in the belly pork. Cook for 15 minutes, sizzling it nicely until it is nearly done. Add the bacon and sizzle this too, then throw in the black pudding – as much as you like – and cook for 5 or 6 minutes, stirring everything from time to time.

Into the pan you tip the broad beans, fresh mint, sugar and wine. Turn up the heat (the Spanish would add a dash of anis here, but I don't care for it). Taste and add a shake of salt, if it's needed, and a few twists of black pepper. Stir well, pop on the lid and cook for 10 minutes more.

Spinach with Raisins and Pine Nuts

Espinacas con Pasas y Piñones

PHOTOGRAPH OPPOSITE PAGE 137

It is harder work being the cameraman on a Floyd shoot than it is being the presenter. My cameraman, the legendary, world-famous Clive North, works extremely hard, and the camera is quite heavy as well.

So it is important that he has three square meals a day. A carefully balanced breakfast comprising fruit juice, cereal and yoghurt, a sensible-sized portion of rashers, eggs, mushrooms and tomatoes, some fresh brown toast and coffee. At lunchtime he prefers to tuck into something substantial yet simple; maybe a couple of T-bone steaks or half-a-dozen lamb chops. But for dinner he likes to prowl round the back streets of whatever city we happen to be in, looking for an interesting restaurant.

And in Barcelona Clive found a little place just round the corner from the Havana Palace Hotel and came back raving about a dish he had had as a starter – Spinach with Raisins and Pine Nuts. In fact, he was not only raving about it, he became absolutely hooked on it and, for the remainder of the shoot, he demanded this easy but tasty dish everywhere he went. So I dedicate this snack to Clive.

Enough for 4 as a starter, or as a side dish to a main meal

50g (2oz) seedless raisins or sultanas
900g (2lb) fresh spinach, thoroughly washed and trimmed
(you could use Swiss chard or kale instead)
3 tablespoons olive oil
1 small clove of garlic, crushed
3 tablespoons pine nuts
Salt
Freshly ground black pepper
Croûtons, to garnish

Pour some boiling water over the raisins or sultanas and leave them to plump up, while you cook the spinach. Do this by packing it into a large saucepan, adding just a little boiling water and a sprinkle of salt. If you have young, tender leaves, then just blanch them for a couple of moments. If you have older spinach, cook it for longer, maybe 10 minutes or so, and chop or shred it so it is more of a mushy mess. The first method is the Chinese way, the second is the Indian. It does depend on whether you have young, succulent spinach leaves. Drain well in a colander, squeezing out the liquid by pressing the spinach down with the back of a spoon. Now chop it roughly.

Heat the oil in a frying pan and sauté the garlic gently for a couple of minutes. Add the spinach, pine nuts and drained, soaked raisins or sultanas. Season with a little more salt if it is needed, and some freshly ground black pepper. Cook gently for about 5 more minutes, then serve with some croûtons sprinkled over.

Sweet Green Pimientos

Pimientos Verdes

Green pimientos, a great delicacy often served for *tapas*, are small green peppers about the size of pullet's eggs, which are dredged in flour, quickly deep-fried and eaten whole with lots of sea salt. I used to eat them by the plateful, especially when I was having one of my non-meat days as I do from time to time. If you can't find the little ones, a passable substitute can be achieved by cutting up the big peppers.

Serves 4

4 large, crunchy, green peppers, cored, seeded and thickly sliced
50g (2oz) plain flour
6 tablespoons olive oil
Sea salt

Take your sliced peppers and dredge them with the flour. Heat the oil in a frying pan and drop in the peppers, a few at a time, stirring them around for a few seconds until they start to look browned and cooked. Remove them from the oil with a slotted spoon and pop them on to kitchen paper to drain. Add plenty of sea salt to taste.

PS Don't add all the peppers to the pan at once, otherwise you will reduce the temperature of the oil too quickly and end up with soggy, greasy pimientos.

Aubergine Fritters

Berenjenas Rehogadas

Serves 4 for *tapas* or main meal accompaniment

1 large shiny aubergine
Salt
4 tablespoons milk
4 tablespoons plain flour
1 teaspoon paprika
Olive oil, for shallow frying

Slice the aubergine thinly and lay out the slices on kitchen paper. Sprinkle liberally with salt and leave for 15 minutes. Turn over the slices and repeat the process. Strain in a colander and dry well with some more kitchen paper. This process draws out the bitter juices from the aubergine and excess moisture so the vegetable cooks crisply.

Dip the slices of aubergine into the milk and then into the flour and paprika, which you have already mixed together and put into a shallow tray.

Now heat the oil in a frying pan, to a depth of about 1cm (a bit less than ½ inch). Quickly fry the aubergine slices until they are crisp. Drain on kitchen paper, sprinkle with salt and enjoy.

PS This is just as delicious with young courgettes, sliced thinly.

Aubergine Purée

Puré de Berenjenas

This brilliant chutney goes well with cold meats or cheese, but is especially good with roast suckling pig or pork.

Makes enough for 4–6, but that depends on your appetite or generosity

5 tablespoons olive oil
2 cloves of garlic, finely chopped
1 large aubergine, cut into chunks
1/4 teaspoon ground cumin
1/4 teaspoon cinnamon
1/4 teaspoon ginger
1/2 teaspoon caster sugar
Finely grated zest of 1/2 lemon
A splash of dry white sherry

Heat the oil in a frying pan and sauté the garlic for a couple of minutes. Throw in the chunks of aubergine and fry gently for about 10 minutes over a medium heat, turning frequently. By this time they will have gone quite soft and pulpy, so they are ready for tipping into your food processor or blender with all the other ingredients. Blend for about 15 seconds or so and serve with Roast Suckling Pig, see page 122.

Potatoes in Garlic Mayonnaise

Patatas en Alioli

Serves 4

675g ($1^1/_2$lb) new potatoes, scrubbed (but not peeled)
4 tablespoons olive oil
2 teaspoons sherry or wine vinegar
Salt
Freshly ground black pepper
7 tablespoons garlic mayonnaise (see page 12)
1 teaspoon paprika

Cook the potatoes in plenty of boiling, lightly salted water until they are tender. Drain them well, then cut into bite-sized pieces.

Mix together the oil and sherry or wine vinegar with a little salt and pepper. Add the garlic mayonnaise and mix in most of the paprika. Add this to the potatoes while they are still warm – this way they will absorb the flavour of the dressing wonderfully. Chill before serving, then sprinkle with the reserved paprika.

Fried Garlic

Ajos Rehogados

This is a brilliant garnish for any grilled meat or fish.

Enough for 2

15 cloves of garlic, peeled
About 1 wineglass dry white wine (enough to cover)
4 tablespoons olive oil

Put the cloves of garlic into a small saucepan and pour over the wine. Simmer gently for about 3 minutes, then drain the garlic and dry on kitchen paper. Heat the oil in a frying pan and toss in the cloves of garlic, frying them briskly until just golden. Heady stuff!

Poor Man's Potatoes

Patatas Pobres

PHOTOGRAPH OPPOSITE PAGE 137

Clive North's favourite Spanish dish, Spinach with Raisins and Pine Nuts, is a Moorish one. But my own favourite, basic meatless recipe has its origins in Peru. In my journeys there are many times when I can't face meat or even fish, but when I find something simple, maybe spicy, comforting – like this dish, Poor Man's Potatoes. For me at least, it is an absolute treat. I like them very hot.

Serves 4

6 tablespoons olive oil
900g (2lb) potatoes, peeled and sliced
Salt
2 cloves of garlic
Black peppercorns – about a dozen will do
1 teaspoon paprika or chilli powder if you like your spuds hot
1 teaspoon ground cumin
3 tablespoons cold water
1 tablespoon white wine vinegar
Chopped fresh parsley, to garnish

Heat the oil in a large frying pan and pop in the sliced potatoes, sprinkling them with some salt. Fry them gently for 8–10 minutes, until they are lightly browned, making sure you turn them over now and again.

In the meantime you can crush the garlic and peppercorns with a mortar and pestle, adding the paprika or chilli, cumin and water to make a paste.

Tip these ingredients in with the potatoes and sprinkle over the vinegar. Stir well and cook for a further 10 minutes or so, until the potatoes are cooked and tender. Serve them piping hot, sprinkled with chopped parsley.

Potatoes with Paprika

Patatas con Paprika

Serves 12 for *tapas* or 6 as a vegetable

12 tablespoons olive oil
6 large old potatoes, cut into thick wedges
Salt
3 teaspoons paprika
3/4 teaspoon cayenne pepper

Pour half the oil into a large shallow casserole dish, or use a roasting pan instead. Put this into a preheated very hot oven, 230°C/450°F (gas mark 8), for a few minutes to get really hot: you want the oil to be just smoking.

Pop the potatoes into the hot oil, arranging them in a single layer. Drizzle over the rest of the olive oil, season with some salt and return to the oven to cook – they will take about 25 minutes.

Mix together the paprika and cayenne pepper and sprinkle over the potatoes. Cook for another 5–10 minutes, when they should be red and crisp on the outside, and fluffy in the middle.

They taste excellent dipped into soured cream or garlic mayonnaise (see page 12).

Potato Casserole

Guiso de Patatas

Serves 4 as a side dish

8 tablespoons olive oil
2 medium onions, chopped
3 cloves of garlic, finely chopped
2 medium tomatoes, skinned and chopped
675g (1 1/2 lb) potatoes, peeled and quartered
1/4 teaspoon cinnamon
1 teaspoon paprika
Salt
250ml (8fl oz) cold water

Heat the oil in a shallow flameproof casserole and sauté the onions and garlic for 3 or 4 minutes, then stir in the tomatoes. Cook for a couple of minutes, then tip in the potatoes and spices. Season with a shake of salt and pour over the water. Continue to cook gently until the potatoes are tender – about 20 minutes, shaking the pan from time to time to prevent the potatoes from sticking.
NB You could use a few strands of saffron instead of the cinnamon and paprika, if you like.

Garlic Purée

Puré de Ajo

The Spanish equivalent to horseradish sauce.

Makes 300ml (½ pint)

12 cloves of garlic, peeled
250ml (8fl oz) white stock
(fish, chicken or veal, as appropriate)
2 tablespoons single cream
Salt
Ground white pepper

Pop the cloves of garlic into a small saucepan and cover with boiling water. Put on the lid and simmer for about 15 minutes, then drain. Crush the cloves of garlic thoroughly with a fork or with a mortar and pestle to make a pulp. It is best, though, to whizz them in a food processor. Put the pulp back into the pan and gradually stir in the stock, then the cream. Taste and season to your liking.

Use the purée to serve alongside fish or white meat, or serve it as a sauce.

Red Stuffed Peppers

Pimientos Morrones Rellenos

When I opened my first little food emporium back in the mid-1960s, one of the most popular dishes was red and green peppers scooped out and stuffed with rice, tomatoes, meat, garlic and herbs. Since then fashions have changed and I hadn't eaten a stuffed pepper for years. They became clichéd in the 1970s when every wine bar served them.

But in the charming little restaurant L'Esclau in Benidorm, stuffed peppers were very much part of the culinary fabric. And Carmen Soriano cooked some for our crew lunch after a busy morning filming the Oven-baked Fish and Potato Pie, which you will find on page 52. This is her recipe. It was delicious, once again because the ingredients benefited from ripening in the Spanish sun and were not those sadly paler, weaker items that we usually find in Northern Europe. So choose ripe, juicy peppers for this dish.

Serves 8 or 4, depending on whether you want one or two each

8 medium red peppers, tops sliced off and seeded

For the sauce

3 tablespoons olive oil
1 medium onion, finely chopped
1 tablespoon tomato purée
1 tablespoon chopped fresh parsley
2 teaspoons plain flour
90ml (3fl oz) vegetable or chicken stock, plus enough to pour round the peppers
150ml (¼ pint) dry white wine

For the stuffing

4 tablespoons olive oil
1 medium onion, finely chopped
1 clove of garlic, finely chopped
225g (8oz) minced beef or lamb
225g (8oz) cooked long-grain rice
1 tablespoon chopped fresh parsley
Salt
Freshly ground black pepper

To make the sauce, heat the oil in a frying pan and sweat the onion for at least 15 minutes, until it is a light golden colour, then stir in the tomato purée, parsley and plain flour. Cook gently for a minute or two, then stir in the stock and white wine and heat until bubbling. Cover and reduce the heat, letting it simmer gently as you get on with the stuffing.

To do that, heat the oil and sizzle together the onion and garlic. Keep the heat on high as you tip in the meat, stirring while it browns. Cook for 5 minutes, then stir in the rice and parsley. Season with some salt and pepper and keep stirring for the next 5 minutes.

Now you have a choice. You can either mix together the sauce and stuffing, fill up the peppers which you have carefully stood upright in a baking dish and then pour in enough water or stock to come halfway up the peppers. Bake in a preheated oven, 190°C/375°F (gas mark 5), until they are ready, or you are ready – about half an hour.

Alternatively, you can fill the peppers with the stuffing only – stood upright in a baking dish as before – and pour the sauce around. Bake at the same temperature for the same time.

Cauliflower Casserole

Guiso de Coliflor

Serves 2 as a main course or 4 as a side dish

1 small cauliflower, broken into florets
5 tablespoons olive oil
1 large onion, chopped
2 cloves of garlic, finely chopped
50g (2oz) pine nuts
50g (2oz) chorizo *sausage, sliced*
25g (1oz) raisins
2 tomatoes, skinned and very finely chopped
1 teaspoon paprika
Salt
2 tablespoons chopped fresh parsley

Cook the cauliflower florets in some lightly salted boiling water for 5–8 minutes. They mustn't get too soft – *al dente* is how you want them, just retaining a bit of bite. Drain really well.

Now heat the oil in a frying pan and add the onion and garlic, frying them for about 5 minutes until golden. Add the pine nuts, *chorizo*, raisins, tomatoes and paprika. Stir well, then add the cauliflower. Cook for a couple of minutes – just enough to heat everything through and mingle the flavours. Season with some salt and serve sprinkled with the parsley.

SALADS

Ensaladas

One of my favourite salads is the ubiquitous *ensalada mixta*, which consists of wonderful crunchy lettuce, slices of sweet Spanish onion, half-green half-red tomatoes sometimes piled high with tuna fish, hard-boiled eggs with rich yellow yolks, and olives. It is simply dressed with sea salt, olive oil and a dash of wine vinegar.

Throughout Spain salads are invariably served as hors d'oeuvres. If you want just a simple green salad to go with your grilled lamb chops or roast leg of lamb you need to speak Spanish pretty damned well.

I have included here a few different kinds of salads that I enjoyed during my trip and I hope you like them too.

Sunshine on a Plate – Salad of Red Peppers with Aubergine and Shallots

Serves 4

6 red peppers
2 medium aubergines
5 tablespoons olive oil
4 shallots, finely chopped
Salt

Put the peppers and aubergines on to a baking sheet and drizzle a few drops of oil over them. Roast them in a preheated fairly hot oven, 200°C/400°F (gas mark 6), for about 20 minutes or so, until the peppers are looking charred and the aubergines are soft. You can do this under the grill, if you prefer, but remember to turn the peppers and aubergines often.

When they have cooled down, peel them. Discard the seeds from the peppers and slice them into strips. Slice the aubergines quite thinly.

Heat 3 tablespoons of the remaining oil in a large frying pan and sauté the shallots until they are soft. Add the aubergines and peppers and stir well, then cook for about 5 minutes, or until they are done to your liking.

Arrange the cooked vegetables attractively on a large plate, drizzling the rest of the oil over them and seasoning with salt.

Chill for at least 1 hour before serving.

Asparagus, La Mancha-Style

Espárragos al Estilo de La Mancha

Makes enough for 2 as a light lunch or
for 4 as an accompaniment

3 tablespoons olive oil
2 cloves of garlic, peeled but not chopped
450g (1lb) asparagus, trimmed –
choose asparagus that isn't too thick

For the sauce
3 egg yolks
$^1/_2$ teaspoon ground cumin
5 teaspoons cold water
Salt
Freshly ground black pepper

Heat the oil in a frying pan big enough to hold the asparagus. Pop in the cloves of garlic first and fry gently until they are beginning to turn brown. Add the asparagus and cook very slowly until tender – about 20–25 minutes.

Mix together all the sauce ingredients and heat carefully until warm. If you heat this mixture too fast or for too long it will curdle. (If you like, you can put the mixture into a heatproof bowl over a pan of simmering water and warm it up this way to prevent curdling.)

When the asparagus is cooked, serve it and eat at once, with the sauce poured over.

Lentil Salad

Ensalada de Lentejas

Serves 4

225g (8oz) brown, green or yellow lentils, soaked and rinsed
1 small onion, peeled and halved
1 carrot, peeled and halved
1 clove of garlic, peeled
2 whole cloves
1 bay leaf
Salt

For the dressing
4 tablespoons olive oil
1 tablespoon red wine vinegar
2 tablespoons minced onion
1 clove of garlic, crushed
2 tablespoons sweet red pepper or pimiento, chopped
Freshly ground black pepper
Salt
3 tablespoons chopped fresh parsley

Put the lentils, onion, carrot, garlic, cloves and bay leaf into a large pot and cover with some salted water. Bring to the boil then reduce the heat and simmer gently with the lid on for about half an hour, until the lentils are just tender. Drain in a colander and rinse. Throw out everything except the lentils and carrot. Chop the carrot into dice, mix with the lentils and transfer to a serving bowl.

Mix together all the ingredients for the dressing, except for the parsley, and pour over the lentils, stirring through gently with a wooden spoon. Allow the salad to stand for an hour or two, so that the lentils absorb the flavour of the dressing. Just before serving, sprinkle over the chopped parsley.

Artichoke and Aubergine, Tomato and Pepper Salad

Serves 4–6 for a starter, 6–7 for *tapas*

1 aubergine, weighing about 225g (8oz)
1 green pepper
1 red pepper
2 average onions
2–3 tablespoons olive oil
3 artichoke hearts (see notes on page 203)
225g (8oz) tomatoes, roughly chopped

For the dressing

4 tablespoons olive oil
3 tablespoons lemon juice
1 clove of garlic, crushed
1 tablespoon chopped fresh parsley
Salt
Freshly ground black pepper

Put the aubergine, peppers and onions into a roasting pan. Drizzle over 2 or 3 tablespoons oil and put them into a preheated oven, 200°C/400°F (gas mark 6), for about half an hour, turning them over a couple of times. Remove from the oven and cover with a sheet of foil to trap the escaping steam, enabling you to peel them more easily. Allow the vegetables to cool and then peel them. Slice the aubergine into strips, remove the seeds from the peppers and slice the flesh, then slice the onions.

Meanwhile, pop the artichoke hearts into a pan of boiling, salted water. Simmer for about 30 minutes, until cooked and tender. Drain, let them cool down and then slice.

Add the artichokes to the aubergine mixture and toss in the tomatoes. Tip it all on to a serving plate.

Mix together all the dressing ingredients – you can do this in a screw-topped jar if you like, giving it a good shake until the oil and lemon juice emulsifies. Pour this brilliant dressing over the salad and chill for a while before serving.

Red Pepper Salad

Ensalada de Pimientos Morrones

We have red peppers all over the place in this book, so here's a recipe for red pepper salad too.

Serves 4–6

4 red peppers
1 clove of garlic, finely chopped

For the dressing

3 tablespoons wine vinegar
Salt
Freshly ground black pepper
6 tablespoons olive oil

Preheat the grill or switch on the oven to 220°C/425°F (gas mark 7). Put the whole peppers under the grill or pop them in the hot oven. Grill or roast for 20–30 minutes until well charred, turning from time to time.

Allow the peppers to cool, then peel them. This is made easier if you cover them with a clean tea towel as soon as you take them from the grill or oven. The steam that is trapped makes the skins softer and easier to peel off. Remove the core and seeds, cut the flesh into long strips and mix with the finely chopped garlic.

Make the dressing by shaking together all the ingredients in a screw-topped jar, not forgetting to put the lid on tight. Pour over the peppers and let them sit in the dressing for a while before serving, to absorb the flavours.

Green Bean Salad

Ensalada de Judías Verdes

Serves 4

450g (1lb) whole green beans, topped and tailed and 'destringed', if necessary
1 medium potato, peeled
1 medium onion, finely chopped

For the dressing

1 clove of garlic, very finely chopped
½ teaspoon ground cumin
6 tablespoons olive oil
3 tablespoons wine vinegar
Salt
Freshly ground black pepper

2 eggs, hard-boiled and sliced
Chopped fresh parsley, coriander or fennel leaves

Cook the beans in plenty of boiling, lightly salted water for about 5 minutes, until they are just tender. Do the same with the potato, except that's going to need about 15–20 minutes, giving you time to make the dressing.

Mix the chopped garlic with the cumin powder, then add the oil and vinegar (you could use lemon juice instead, of course). Season and mix well.

Refresh the cooked beans in cold water, drain throughly and arrange on a plate. Slice the cooked potato and pop the pieces in among the beans, then scatter the chopped onion over the top. Drizzle with the dressing and garnish with sliced eggs and a sprinkling of chopped herbs.

Rice Salad

Ensalada de Arroz

Serves 4 as a starter or accompaniment

450g (1lb) cooked long-grain rice – brown or white, whatever you prefer
1 onion, finely chopped
1 clove of garlic, finely minced
1 green pepper, cored, seeded and finely chopped
10 black olives, pitted and chopped
10 green olives, pitted and chopped
2 tablespoons chopped fresh parsley
Salt
Freshly ground black pepper
6 tablespoons olive oil
3 tablespoons wine or sherry vinegar
Anchovy fillets, to garnish

Stir the rice through to make sure that the grains are separate and fluffed up, then throw in the onion, garlic, pepper, olives and chopped parsley. Add some salt and grind in a little pepper, then mix everything together really well.

To make the dressing: mix together the oil and vinegar, with a little salt and pepper. Shake up these ingredients in a screw-topped jar, if you like. Pour over the rice salad and toss it through. Garnish with thin strips of anchovy fillet, and serve.

EGGS, GRAINS AND PASTA

Potato Omelette

Tortilla Española

Fourteen-year-old beach bar cooks can make *tortillas* to perfection. All grannies – Spanish ones that is – can make them to perfection. And yet, seemingly the simplest of dishes, it is one of the most difficult in which to achieve perfection. Do not make the mistake of thinking it is just fried potatoes with egg over the top.

The secret lies in having a heavy, well-used iron frying pan and in using the finest-quality olive oil and chunks of extremely waxy potatoes. And then in cooking those potatoes in a generous amount of the oil for a long time, so that they have absorbed the flavour of the oil and are neither falling apart nor raw hard cubes. The potatoes are almost rather boiled more than fried in the oil.

Most important of all, when the *tortilla* is cooked, it must be eaten – after it has been allowed to sit for half an hour or so – like a slice of cake. It is also delicious served cold later in the day as a *tapa*. Remember, these kinds of omelettes were made for people to take to work for their mid-morning break or their lunch in the fields or factories. Show me a good Spanish omelette-maker and I will show you a sensitive cook. It is not a dish to play or joke with.

250g (8 fl oz) olive oil
4 large potatoes, peeled and cut into chunks
1 medium onion, thinly sliced
Salt
4 large eggs, beaten

Heat the oil in a frying pan – do use olive oil, otherwise your *tortilla* will be a poor relation to anything the Spaniards cook. Add the potatoes, a handful at a time, and then the onion. Stir well and season with a good sprinkling of salt.

Cook gently for about 20 minutes or so. The general idea is to stew the potatoes in the oil, rather than to get them brown and crisp. Stir them from time to time and if you find they have 'caked', just break them up gently. When they are cooked, remove the potatoes from the pan. Pour out the oil and reserve it. Mix the potatoes with the beaten eggs and season with a bit more salt.

Wipe out the frying pan with some kitchen paper, then reheat 2 tablespoons of the reserved oil, until it is really hot. Tip in the potato mixture. Lower the heat and shake the pan frequently to prevent sticking. Cook gently until the potatoes begin to brown underneath and the mixture is set. Next, find a plate the same size as the frying pan and pop it over the pan. Flip the whole lot over – you should now have your *tortilla* on the plate, with the cooked side uppermost.

Add 1 more tablespoon of oil to the pan and slide the omelette back in (do this with confidence, it is always the best way). Cook the *tortilla* for another 4–5 minutes, or until it is brown on the second side.

Serve in wedges. Simple, but truly wonderful! Try it at lukewarm temperature, as the Spanish do, or even cold with pickles and chutney.

Flamenco Eggs

Huevos Flamencos

This is a Spanish version of *oeufs cocotte*. It is a sunny, spicy dish that would make a perfect starter for a party or a wonderful light lunch. By the way, the point of using tinned pimientos is that they are effectively already cooked and so are only heated up in these little *cocottes*. If you used fresh peppers you would have to precook them and though this is a nice dish, I don't think it merits that much trouble.

Serves 4

You will need 4 individual shallow ovenproof dishes

300ml (½ pint) fresh tomato sauce (see page 13)
8 eggs
4 tablespoons peas or chopped green beans, cooked
1 dozen asparagus tips, cooked (the Spanish seem to adore tinned asparagus – I think it's dreadful. The choice is yours)
1 × 200g (7oz) can pimientos, well drained and sliced
150g (5oz) serrano *ham, diced*
8 slices of spicy sausage, ideally chorizo
½ teaspoon paprika
1 tablespoon chopped fresh parsley
Salt
Freshly ground black pepper

Divide the tomato sauce equally between each ovenproof dish, then crack two eggs into each one. Toss over the peas or beans. Arrange the asparagus, pimiento, ham and spicy sausage around the eggs, then sprinkle over the paprika and parsley. Season with salt and pepper.

Pop these into a preheated oven, 200°C/400°F (gas mark 6), for about 10 minutes, or until the egg whites are set but the yolks are still soft. Scrumptious with triangles of fried bread.

Opposite: Mixed Vegetables, Spanish-Style (page 144)
Next page, from left to right: Beef and Potato Hotpot (page 109); Galician Stew (page 26); Chilled Garlic and Almond Soup with Grapes (page 22)

Scrambled Eggs with Seafood

Huevos Revueltos con Mariscos

We drove along the drab coastal strip out of Málaga looking for this restaurant that they said was third on the right, not far along. After an hour and a half of one-way systems, unfinished fly-overs and dual carriageways that ended abruptly in a mountain of road-building materials, in a hot little car (why don't Spanish hire cars have air conditioning, it is a bloody hot country after all), tempers were overheating.

Anyway, to cut a long story short, we finally found the restaurant; it was damned obvious and we should have seen it on our first fly-past. The village itself, El Palo, was quite ordinary, but from the moment I stepped inside La Refectorium I knew we had hit on a good one. The waiters were leisurely delivering mountains of food to chic Spanish women in gold shoes – in fact, if gold hadn't been invented I have no idea what Spanish women would wear – and coiffured men in crisp white shirts, ties loose round collars, jackets on shoulders. It is a restaurant of carefully understated style. You smell the food and not the fat. And each table is adorned with a vase of irises and cornflowers. Perspiring legs of cured ham swing from the ceiling, each with its little upside-down Aladdin's hat pegged underneath to catch the drips.

We were greeted warmly. We gulped down a few iced drinks they brought us, nibbled some really nutty sweet olives, followed by thin slivers of exquisite *serrano* ham. Then the most extraordinary thing happened. The owner came up to take our order and, for something like four minutes, I babbled in completely fluent Spanish with him, whereas the day before I hadn't even been able to order a beer without breaking into French. He offered us hake and clams, dishes in aspic and salt, octopus or whatever, but what we needed was something simple. So we had plates of tiny lamb chops from milk-fed lamb, which were charred black on the outside but were juicy and pink inside. We picked each one up by the little bone and chomped it. And the chips were splendid too, deep-fried in olive oil. We also had one of those crunchy salads that the Spanish do so well – crisp little slivers of

Left Sponge Cake with Nuts and Cherries (page 197);
Right Santiago Cake (page 196)

onion, sliced red tomatoes and green peppers, a pinch of salt and a dash of olive oil, a dash of vinegar.

After the dessert, one of my favourites, Prune Ice Cream with Armagnac (see page 192), some 1860 Spanish brandy, and cups of strong black espresso. Then we had some more 1860 brandy. I nibbled away, because I have a sweet tooth, on some *turrón*, a kind of honey and almond nougat (see page 199). In fact, memories have come flooding back as I dictate this to Anne, who was also at the lunch with me, and I am going to have a piece now. Hmmm! Delicious!

However, I digress. I have led you up a cul-de-sac actually because we were at La Refectorium to film a cooking sketch and this is the delectable dish I prepared. It is particularly good if you are able to use free-range eggs, which give that elusive taste of the countryside that merges harmoniously with the slightly salt taste of the sea through the prawns. Like all food, dull eggs and dull prawns equal a dull dish!

PS The wine we drank was a Yllera red.

Serves 1

1 tablespoon olive oil
1–2 cloves of garlic, finely chopped
50–75g (2–3oz) seafood – I used half-a-dozen prawns, peeled up to the tail and last joint
50g (2oz) dwarf runner beans, sliced and precooked for 3–4 minutes in some boiling water
25g (1oz) serrano *ham, finely diced*
Salt
Freshly ground black pepper
3 eggs, beaten

Heat the oil in a non-stick saucepan and add the chopped garlic, frying it until it is golden – about 2–3 minutes. Stir in the prawns – or whatever seafood you could lay your hands on – and cook until they're done. A couple of minutes should do nicely. Toss in the beans and ham and perhaps just a little salt and a twist or two of pepper. Add the eggs, cook until lightly scrambled and tip them on to a warmed plate. You'll never want 'normal' scrambled eggs again.

Piparrada

Piparrada is an egg and vegetable dish common to the Spanish and French living on both sides of the Pyrenees, the Basque people. And though it is a simple concoction of peppers and tomatoes stir-fried with eggs and sometimes enriched with pieces of grilled mountain ham and is absolutely dead easy to do, I can never make it without recalling the time I cooked it near St Jean-de-Luz for an aristocratic French lady called Mimi in the television series, *Floyd on France.*

I was very anxious to impress this *grande dame* and quite literally over-egged the omelette. 'That's not a *pipérade*,' she said, 'it's more like scrambled egg with traffic lights.' (She was referring to the red, yellow and green peppers I had stirred into it.)

It is very important, to reach Mimi's standards, to cook the vegetables first so they are soft, tender and succulent, and then whisk in the finest of free-range eggs so you have a wonderful mound of yellow, frothy scrambled egg dotted, like some Spanish crown, with the colours of the culinary trilogy.

Serves 4

4 tablespoons olive oil
1 medium onion, finely chopped
3 cloves of garlic, finely chopped
1 × 200g (7oz) can pimientos, drained and chopped
225g (8oz) tomatoes, skinned and chopped
100g (4oz) serrano *ham, chopped*
8 eggs
Salt
Freshly ground black pepper
Triangles of fried bread, to serve

Heat the oil in a large frying pan and add the onion and garlic. Fry gently for about 3 minutes until softened, then stir in the pimientos, tomatoes and ham. Cook gently for 3 or 4 minutes, stirring from time to time. This gives you plenty of time to whisk up the eggs, seasoning with salt and pepper. Pour the eggs into the frying pan and cook for about 30 seconds to set them lightly before you scramble them – don't let them get too dry. Tip out on to warm serving plates and serve with the fried bread.

Migas

PHOTOGRAPH OPPOSITE PAGE 40

On our journey from Málaga to Madrid via Granada and Toledo, to name but two, we travelled by bus (actually We didn't travel by bus, The crew did). I pottered along in my works Bentley and waved at them as they dropped off at the Transport Café for lunch while I checked out the best place in town.

It all sounds simple and pleasant enough but the bus was not only used for transporting all the crew and their equipment, it also occasionally had to star in our programmes.

And all this must really have tried the patience of our driver, Rafael. I am sure he won't mind if I call him plump, for plump he was. But no request, whatever it was, was too much for him. He would drive over a mountain so we could be filmed *in situ*, or drive up a track which normally wouldn't take anything other than a military vehicle, or drive round and round the block as we tried to follow some utterly impossible directions – in short, the man was a saint.

So to celebrate his goodness, the director suggested I could cook him a wonderful, extravagant, stupendous meal.

'Shall we do lobster, or perhaps partridge?' said I.

'No, no,' he said, 'cook him a *migas*.'

Generous to a fault we were . . . If you were to look up *migas* in a Spanish dictionary, you would probably be disappointed to find it means 'fried breadcrumbs'. Luckily, its literal translation bears little resemblance to this wonderful dish, originally eaten out of poverty, but now out of choice.

Serves 4

375g (14oz) stale bread, crusts removed and cut into cubes
2 tablespoons cold water
3 tablespoons olive oil
100g (4oz) bacon, chopped
3 cloves of garlic, chopped
1 teaspoon paprika
1/4 teaspoon ground cumin (or a hefty pinch)
Salt
Freshly ground black pepper
1 small onion, finely chopped
50g (2oz) serrano *ham, chopped (or buy* prosciutto *instead)*
4 eggs, for frying (more if you're hungry)

Right – put the cubes of bread in a bowl and sprinkle the water over the top, stirring well. Cover and set aside.

Heat 2 tablespoons of the oil in a large, heavy-based frying pan. Add the bacon and cook until it is fairly crisp. Lift out with a slotted spoon and set this aside too. Now add 1 clove of chopped garlic to the pan and cook until brown. Fish it out and discard.

Go back to the bread and season it with the paprika and cumin, then some salt and pepper. Mix it well, then add to the frying pan over a very low heat. The idea is to cook it very slowly for about 20 minutes, stirring from time to time, without browning.

Meanwhile, heat the remaining tablespoon of oil in a separate pan and sauté the onion for a few minutes until soft. Add the rest of the garlic and cook for a couple of minutes longer. Pop in the *serrano* ham and the bacon you cooked earlier, stir everything together and cook for 2 minutes to heat through.

When the bread is done, tip the onion mixture into it, stirring well. Quickly make some fried eggs, which taste superb with this mixture, and serve it to whomever. They will soon be confirmed *migas* addicts, like my chum Rafael.

Mountain Breakfast

Desayuno de Montaña

PHOTOGRAPH OPPOSITE PAGE 40

Pork and beans or sausage and beans is a popular classic – from the John Wayne camp fire cowboy-type to the great British banger and a tin of Heinz beans to the outstanding French *cassoulet.* Pork and beans or any combination thereof is always a winner.

We spent a few days mountain-biking up in the Sierra Nevada and, with limited cooking facilities, I ensured that my pannier bag always carried some spicy Spanish sausage, which keeps well without refrigeration, smoked ham and a couple of jars of plainly cooked white beans. Believe me, if you have had plenty of exercise, a frying pan sizzling with sausages, pork and beans over a camp fire in the fresh morning sets you up 'proper good' (please use Devonian accent) for the day.

I cooked this little snack high on a mountain on a clear but chilly day near the town of Bubión. And in the pale blue distance I could just see the coast of North Africa (he lied, with a light smile playing upon his fat and fulsome lips).

Enough for 2, or 1 large appetite

2 tablespoons olive oil
2 red peppers, cored, seeded and sliced
2–3 cloves of garlic, chopped
2–3 chorizo, *sliced*
2 morcilla *(Spanish black sausage) or use about 175g (6oz) black pudding, sliced*
175g (6oz) canned haricot beans, drained
Freshly ground black pepper

Heat the oil in a pan and sizzle together the red peppers and garlic to get your tastebuds really going, then add the sausages and cook for about 5–8 minutes. Stir in the beans and pepper and bubble them up, then cook gently until you can't wait any longer for your breakfast – 5 minutes is time enough.

Macaroni with Spicy Sausage and Tomato

Macaroni a la Española

Serves 4

225g (8oz) macaroni
3 tablespoons olive oil
1 onion, chopped
1 large green pepper, cored, seeded and chopped
2 cloves of garlic, finely chopped
4 medium tomatoes, skinned and chopped
100g (4oz) serrano *ham, chopped*
*3 spicy sausages (*chorizo, *if possible), sliced*
Freshly ground black pepper
Salt
100g (4oz) Cheddar-type cheese, grated

Cook the macaroni in lots of lightly salted boiling water, for about 8 minutes until it is tender, then drain well.

While the macaroni is cooking, heat the oil in a frying pan and sauté together the onion, pepper and garlic until softened, about 10 minutes, then stir in the tomatoes. Add the ham and sausage and heat through, giving it a good stir. Season with some black pepper. Taste it and, if necessary, add some salt. You may not need any because the ham is quite salty.

Add this mixture to the cooked macaroni and stir through. Transfer to a heatproof serving dish. Sprinkle the surface liberally with the cheese, then melt it under a preheated hot grill and cook until bubbling and golden – approximately 5 minutes.

Traditional Paella

Paella takes its name from the shallow-sided, two-handled frying pan in which it is cooked. In former times the paellas were made from earthenware, but steel ones are more common these days. You will need one at least 24 inches in diameter to make enough for four to six people.

Spanish restaurants have paellas up to 8 feet in diameter. The very biggest one I ever saw was in Benidorm; it must have been 30 feet in diameter, certainly large enough to feed 1,500 people. It was absolutely fascinating to watch five or six cooks literally shovelling rice into this monster pan and throwing in buckets of tomatoes and snails and bucket after bucket of chopped rabbit and chicken. It was just a little party Benidorm puts on once or twice a year to cheer up the visitors. It certainly cheered us up.

Depending on what part of Spain you are in, you will either find meat- or fish-based paellas, or indeed both. Paellas, by the way, are usually eaten for lunch. The recipe I include here is a typical Valencian one made from rabbit, chicken or both, but in other areas they may well add mussels, shrimps, prawns and clams. It is also a question of expense. Snails are often added to the Valencian paella – which doesn't have fish by the way. It is up to you whether or not you use snails. On the bottom line you can put in anything you like.

But whether it is a meat or fish paella, there will always be some kind of vegetable in it, normally fresh peas or beans or dried but cooked beans. Its unique flavour comes from the saffron that is added. Cheapskate cooks pop in turmeric but that only serves to colour it, barely flavouring it in the authentic way.

It was the Arabs who introduced rice to Spain. If they hadn't, I suppose paella wouldn't have been invented. Incidentally, Spain is one of the largest producers of rice in Europe, and the best paellas are made from short-grain rice that has been well-washed and strained before using. A good paella is cooked so that the bottom of the rice forms a crust, not burnt but golden and crunchy. In modern Spain paellas range from pre-prepared, individually frozen portions to mountains of rice with about one prawn or two peas in it to, happily more often than not, a steaming mountain of aromatic rice, meat and vegetables, lovingly cooked. A truly great feast.

Serves 4–6

1.25–1.5kg (3–3½lb) chicken or rabbit or both, jointed into small pieces
Salt
Freshly ground black pepper
6 tablespoons olive oil
2 cloves of garlic, finely chopped
175g (6oz) peas
225g (8oz) green beans – runner or French, chopped into 2.5cm (1 inch) pieces, or cooked broad beans or cooked white haricot beans or all three
4 large tomatoes, skinned and chopped
1 tablespoon paprika
450g (1lb) short-grain rice
Few strands of saffron
1.2 litres (2 pints) chicken stock
12 snails, cleaned (optional)
2 lemons, cut into wedges, to garnish

Season the chicken or rabbit with some salt and pepper. Heat up the oil in a large paella or frying pan, add the chicken (or rabbit) and sauté for about 10 minutes, turning frequently. Add the garlic, peas, beans and tomatoes. Sprinkle in the paprika, add the rice, saffron and stock and bring to the boil. Add the snails if using, then reduce the heat and bubble gently for about 30 minutes, until the rice is cooked and the liquid has been absorbed.

Take the pan off the heat and cover for 5 minutes – this will fluff up the rice. Garnish with wedges of lemon and serve with a decent bottle of wine.

Paella with Noodles

Paella con Fideos

In the sleepy village of Tarbena just a few miles from Benidorm – that open-air asylum of fun, food and drink and, of course, capitalism – there is a restaurant called Casa Pinet, which is a veritable shrine to Communism.

The one-armed, bereted patron, Jerónimo Pinet, is a dedicated Communist. His walls are adorned with statues of Marx and Che Guevara and revolutionary posters, with effigies of Thatcher and Reagan hanging in nooses from the beams of this little fun palace. Any house music is invariably the *Internationale* rather than *Viva España*! I don't know how serious a Communist Jerónimo is – it seems a bit of an occupation passé to my mind – but people flock to his doors to enjoy the food. One of the dishes the restaurant specialises in is paella with a sort of macaroni or *bucatini*, the hollow stuff you find in Italy, broken into one-inch pieces.

According to Señora Pinet, this unique dish was accidentally discovered by some local fishermen who put to sea in a badly-provisioned boat. When it was time for the cook to prepare the food of the day, which was probably rice with whatever fish they had caught, to his dismay and horror he found there was no rice. All he had was some of this macaroni, but since he had forgotten to bring milk, butter and cheese, he couldn't even make a macaroni cheese. And so this superb dish was created.

Señora Pinet cooked it in a proper paella pan, about six feet in diameter and for the few hours I was at the restaurant dozens of people ordered it and only empty plates came back. It is an extremely pleasant variation of a classic theme.

Serves 6–8

For the *picada*
2 tablespoons olive oil
2 cloves of garlic, crushed
50g (2oz) almonds
1 slice of bread
2 tablespoons fresh chopped parsley
Few strands of saffron
4 tablespoons olive oil

150ml (1/4 pint) tomato sauce (see page 13)
175g (6oz) squidlets (small squid) cleaned and chopped
175g (6oz) mixed white fish – choose from hake, monkfish, grouper, cod etc., cut into chunks
50g (2oz) mussels, well scrubbed (throw out any damaged ones

or ones that remain shut when tapped)
100g (4oz) clams, well scrubbed
(again, throw out any damaged ones)
100g (4oz) small prawns in shells
3 tomatoes, skinned and chopped
1 red pepper, cored, seeded and chopped
100g (4oz) peas
175g (6oz) fresh tuna steak, cut into chunks
Salt
Freshly ground black pepper
1.2 litres (2 pints) fish stock
450g (1lb) thin noodles or macaroni

For the garnish
Mussels
Large prawns in their shells
Red peppers, cooked separately in olive oil
Lemon wedges

First of all, make the *picada* by heating the 2 tablespoons of oil and gently sautéeing the garlic and almonds for 3 or 4 minutes. Remove with a draining spoon and put them on to some kitchen paper. Fry the slice of bread until golden and crisp. Break it up and pop it into a food processor or blender with the garlic, almonds, parsley and saffron, whizzing everything together for a few moments to make a smooth *picada* (used later for thickening, flavouring and enriching the dish).

Now heat the 4 tablespoons of oil in a very large pan. Add the tomato sauce and cook for a few moments, while you keep stirring. Add the squidlets and cook for a couple of minutes. Next, the mixed white fish, followed by the mussels, clams, prawns, tomatoes, pepper and peas. Keep on cooking over a gentle heat, then add the chunks of fresh tuna steak. Add some salt and pepper and stir the *picada* into the pot.

Pour in the fish stock and add the pasta. Bubble on a low heat for about 20 minutes, when the pasta will be cooked. Give everything a thorough stir, and transfer to a huge serving platter.

Garnish with cooked mussels and large prawns arranged around the dish, then the red peppers (which you remembered to fry separately in oil). Finally, a few lemon wedges scattered for a flourish of colour.

Rice on the Side

Arroz a Banda

Arroz a banda means rice on its own – abandoned rice. It is one of those dishes born out of the poverty of former times when perhaps the family income only supported the purchase of basic goods. The inventive housekeeper would maybe buy a fish head to make some soup or stock with which to flavour that constant staple, rice. For a special treat, some inexpensive pieces of squid would be thrown in, as an apology for the mountains of prawns and mussels that the booted and horsed classes would eat.

Like so many simple dishes born from necessity, it is quite delicious. It is virtually a fishless, meatless paella. The rich fish stock enriches and infuses the rice.

Serves 4

For the *picada*
6 tablespoons olive oil
1 dried sweet red pepper, cored, seeded and chopped
2 cloves of garlic, chopped
Few strands of saffron
Salt
Freshly ground black pepper

225g (8oz) fresh squidlets (small squid), cleaned and chopped
3 tablespoons fresh tomato sauce (see page 13)
325g (12oz) short-grain rice
1.2 litres (2 pints) good fish stock – this is very important (see page 16)

To make the *picada*, heat the oil in a very large paella or frying pan. Cook together the pepper and garlic for 2 or 3 minutes, then transfer them to a blender, reserving the oil. Add the saffron to them with some salt and pepper and blend until smooth. Reserve until later.

Add the squidlets to the pan and fry them briefly, then stir in the fresh tomato sauce. Tip in the rice and add the fish stock. No compromises here, I'm afraid, you must use a really good fish stock, which of course you will have if you've followed my recipe on page 16. The essence of this dish is that it tastes of the sea, without actually containing much seafood.

Add the red pepper *picada* to the pan and stir through, then cook gently for about 20–25 minutes, until the rice is cooked and tender and the liquid has been absorbed.

Serve this wondrously simple and satisfying dish with a bowl of garlic mayonnaise, a recipe for which you will find on page 12.

Moors and Christians – Black Beans and White Rice

Moros y Christianos

Spain has a passionate, bloody and glorious past. Ironically, the wars with successive waves of invaders, which caused so much devastation at the time, have helped to mould Spain into one of the most culturally and gastronomically rich countries of the world. Add to that the influences that resulted from the discovery of the Americas and you have a glorious bubbling pot of flavours, tastes and textures.

But, of course, while ethnic and religious influences dictate what people eat, poverty and wealth also play their part. Here is a whimsical meat-free recipe that typifies the ultimate harmony Spain managed to achieve between Moors and Christians. It is a simple dish of rice and beans that I ate in Benidorm of all places on the evening of their spectacular Moors, Christians and Visigoths festival, where the burghers of Benidorm, clad in the most exquisite costumes, paraded to the vibrant throb of big drums. I was told that there is a long waiting list to join the Moors Society because their costumes are more brilliant than the Christian ones. So once a year for one evening everyone dresses up as Charlton Heston and Sophia Loren. Or was it Cary Grant and Sophia Loren in the film based on *The Gun* by C.S. Forester, which they retitled *The Pride and the Passion*. Flashing black-eyed Spanish beauties smile alluringly, macho men puff on fat cigars and the power and glory that Spain once was manifests itself.

PS I want to be a big star in a major Moors and Christians epic!

Now for the recipe:

Moors and Christians

Serves 4–6

225g (8oz) black kidney beans, soaked overnight, then drained
600ml (1 pint) cold water
1 onion, chopped into 4
1 large carrot, sliced in half
1 stick of celery, sliced in half
3–4 cloves of garlic, peeled but not chopped
1 bay leaf
1 teaspoon paprika
Juice of 1 orange
2 tablespoons olive oil
2 shallots, finely chopped
225g (8oz) tomatoes, skinned and chopped
1 small green pepper, cored, seeded and chopped
Salt
Freshly ground black pepper
225g (8oz) long-grain rice
2 tablespoons chopped fresh parsley
Finely sliced onion, orange, hard-boiled egg and banana, to garnish

Bring the beans to the boil in the water and cook rapidly for 15 minutes – this is important, because dried kidney beans (both red and black) contain toxins on the outer skin when raw. Add the onion, carrot, celery, garlic and bay leaf to the pan. Partially cover the pan and simmer gently until the beans are almost done – about 1½ hours. Check from time to time on the water level, topping up if necessary. Stir in the paprika and orange juice and finish off the cooking. Drain the beans and remove the onion, carrot, celery, garlic and bay leaf.

Heat the oil in a small frying pan and sauté the shallots, tomatoes and pepper for about 15 minutes. Stir this mixture through the beans.

Cook the rice for about 12 minutes in plenty of boiling, salted water. Drain it, then pack it quite firmly into a buttered ring mould, if you have one. If not, you'll have to make do with a pudding basin.

Arrange the black bean mixture on a large serving dish and unmould the rice ring on top. Garnish with the bits and pieces.

Rice with Nuts and Garlic

Arroz con Nueces y Ajo

I know I am perceived by many to be an out-and-out carnivore who between guzzling vast quantities of wine sneers at vegetarians, but this isn't really true. Because eating and cooking plays such a large part in my life there are many times in the week when the thought of red meat makes my stomach turn. And out of kindness to my stomach, liver and digestive system in general, I very often enjoy meat-free food. This pleasant rice dish, with the Moorish influence of nuts, is a real cracker. I would recommend, though, that you use wild or basmati rice.

Serves 6

40g (1½oz) walnuts, chopped
4 cloves of garlic, crushed
3 tablespoons chopped fresh parsley
75g (3oz) hard cheese, whatever you like, grated
5 tablespoons olive oil
Salt
Freshly ground black pepper
900ml (1½ pints) chicken or vegetable stock
Juice of ½ large lemon
325g (12oz) long-grain rice

Ideally, you need quite a large pestle and mortar to start off this recipe so you can pulverise the walnuts with the garlic and parsley to make a paste. You could easily throw everything into your blender instead, but it won't achieve quite the right texture. (This only matters if you are a perfectionist.)

When you have the paste, stir in the grated cheese, then pour in the oil in a thin stream, beating all the time. Season to taste. Bring the stock to the boil in a large saucepan. Add the lemon juice and tip in the rice. Pop on the lid, lower the heat and simmer for 15–20 minutes, until the rice is cooked. (Check to make sure it doesn't boil dry.)

Drain the rice well and put it into a large bowl that you have warmed up. Check the seasonings – especially the pepper (there should be plenty). Stir through the nut and garlic mixture and serve.

Cannelloni, Catalan-Style

Canelones a la Catalana

Serves 4

8 large fresh or dried pasta squares

For the filling

2 tablespoons olive oil
1 large onion, finely chopped
2 cloves of garlic, crushed
225g (8oz) lean minced beef
225g (8oz) lean minced pork
1 tablespoon brandy
50g (2oz) fresh white breadcrumbs
1 tablespoon chopped fresh parsley
Salt
Freshly ground black pepper

For the sauce

50g (2oz) butter
50g (2oz) plain flour
600ml (1 pint) milk
Salt
Freshly ground black pepper

For the topping

100g (4oz) hard cheese, grated

To make the filling, heat the oil in a large saucepan and fry the onion and garlic for about 3 or 4 minutes until softened. Add the meat, a handful at a time, stirring well between each addition so that it browns and sizzles. Continue to cook it gently for about 10–15 minutes, then remove from the heat. Stir in the brandy, breadcrumbs and parsley and season with some salt and pepper. When it has cooled a little, whizz it all together in your food processor or blender to make a smooth mince.

If you are using dried pasta, then cook it according to the pack instructions. Pipe or spoon the mince mixture on to the pasta in horizontal lines (José Ceres did this expertly). Roll up the pasta and line them up in a buttered ovenproof dish.

Make the sauce by melting the butter, then adding the flour and cooking it for a minute to make a *roux*. Gradually add the milk, then heat it until the sauce boils and thickens. Cook for a minute or so, season with some salt and pepper and pour over the pasta.

Strew the grated cheese all over the surface then pop the dish into a preheated oven, 200°C/400°F (gas mark 6). It will need 30–40 minutes, by which time it will be golden brown and bubbling.

Puddings, Cakes and Drinks

Pears in Red Wine

Peras en Vino Tinto

Serves 6

6 medium pears – choose ones that aren't too ripe
500ml (16fl oz) dry red wine
150ml (1/4 pint) water
3 tablespoons brown sugar
3 tablespoons clear honey
Pared zest of 1/2 lemon (use a potato peeler to do this)
Pared zest of 1/2 orange
1 × 5cm (2 inch) piece of cinnamon stick

Leave the stems on the pears and keep them whole. Now peel them.

Put all the remaining ingredients into a medium saucepan and heat gently to dissolve the sugar and honey. Pop the pears into the pan and simmer very gently with the lid on, spooning the liquid over the pears from time to time until they are tender – about 15 minutes.

Transfer the pears to a serving dish. Bubble the liquid for about 5 minutes to reduce it so that it is syrupy, then pour it over the pears. Fish out the zest and cinnamon stick. Allow the syrup time to cool down, then pop the dish into the fridge to chill before serving.

Cheesecake

Pastel de Queso

Makes 1 × 20cm (8 inch) cake

For the dough

175g (6oz) plain flour
Pinch of salt
45g (1½oz) cold butter, diced
2½ tablespoons cold water

For the filling

2 eggs
225g (8oz) cream cheese
(you could use ricotta or cottage cheese instead)
75g (3oz) caster sugar
2 tablespoons clear honey
½ teaspoon ground cinnamon

This is a sort of flat cheesecake popular in Ibiza. Start off by sifting the flour and salt into a bowl. Rub in the diced butter until the mixture looks like fine breadcrumbs, then stir in enough water to make a stiff dough.

Roll this out on a lightly floured surface into a rectangle, then fold up the dough into three, as if you were folding up a letter to go in an envelope. Roll out and fold twice more, then roll out and use to line a 20cm (8 inch) flan dish or ring, placed on a baking sheet.

Next, make the filling by beating together all the ingredients, except the cinnamon. Pour into the flan case and level the surface. Bake in a preheated oven, 180°C/350°F (gas mark 4), for about 45 minutes, until the filling is set.

Let the cheesecake cool down, then sprinkle over the cinnamon.

Gypsy Arm Roll

Brazo de Gitano

Spanish Swiss roll – geddit, ho ho ho!

Makes 1 roll, about 8 slices

For the cake

4 eggs, separated
75g (3oz) caster sugar
75g (3oz) plain flour
1 teaspoon finely grated lemon zest
3 tablespoons icing sugar

For the filling

2 egg yolks
2 tablespoons caster sugar
1 tablespoon cornflour
Pinch of salt
225ml (7½ fl oz) milk
2 teaspoons vanilla essence
1 small piece cinnamon stick
2 tablespoons cold water
1 tablespoon butter

First find a Swiss roll tin measuring about 25 × 37cm (10 × 15 inches). Grease it, line it with baking parchment or greaseproof paper and grease again.

Next, separate the eggs into two large bowls – preferably metal ones. Add two-thirds of the caster sugar to the egg yolks and whisk them, with the bowl placed over a pan of hot water, using a balloon whisk, electric beater or egg beater, until the mixture is really thick and pale – about 5 minutes should do it. You will know that it is right when you lift the beaters out of the mixture and the impression is left for several seconds.

Now whisk the egg whites – don't forget to clean the beaters first – until they hold stiff peaks. Add the rest of the caster sugar and whisk again until the whites are glossy – about 30 seconds more.

Using a spatula or metal spoon, fold the egg whites and flour, with the lemon zest, into the egg yolk mixture in three alternate batches, doing it as lightly as you possibly can. Pour this cake mixture into your prepared tin, tilting it so it covers the surface evenly. Pop into a preheated hot oven, 220°C/425°F (gas mark 7), for 8–10 minutes until well-risen, golden brown and spongy to touch.

While it is in the oven, find a large sheet of baking parchment or greaseproof paper, just a bit bigger than the Swiss roll tin, and sift a little icing sugar on to it. When the cake is cooked, turn it out right away on to this paper, peel off the lining paper then cut off the crusty edges quickly. Roll up the cake from the long edge with the paper inside. Let it cool down completely while you make the filling.

Put the egg yolks, caster sugar, cornflour and a pinch of salt into a medium bowl. Heat the milk with the vanilla essence and cinnamon stick until almost boiling, then let it cool down for a few minutes. Fish out the cinnamon stick. Whisk this milk into the egg yolk mixture, then place the bowl over a pan of gently simmering water. Stir until thickened and smooth, add the water and cook gently for about 10 minutes. Remove from the heat and beat in the butter. The mixture should now be smooth and silky. Let it cool down before you use it.

Unroll the cake, spread over the delicious custard filling and roll up again – without the paper inside this time. Sprinkle with the rest of the icing sugar.

Leche Frita

You may remember the story about dinner for the President of Galicia (see page 49)? Well, after all that, the crew went off to another of our friend Moncho's restaurants for dinner. I, of course, was too exhausted and had to prepare for the next day's filming. They all came back raving about Fried Milk or Leche Frita. I said I'd take their word for it. But dubious though it may sound, I later found it truly is extremely tasty – and a great Spanish favourite.

Serves 6

100g (4oz) caster sugar
65g (2½oz) cornflour
2 eggs, plus 2 egg yolks
500ml (16fl oz) milk
Pared zest of ½ lemon
Pared zest of ½ orange
1 cinnamon stick

For the coating

1 large egg, beaten
2 tablespoons cold water
A few handfuls of fresh white breadcrumbs
Vegetable oil, for shallow frying – or half oil and half butter
2 tablespoons caster sugar
½ teaspoon ground cinnamon

In a large mixing bowl, whisk together the sugar, cornflour, eggs and egg yolks until blended. Heat the milk in a heavy-based saucepan with the lemon and orange zest and the cinnamon stick. When it reaches boiling point, remove the pan from the heat and just let it sit there for about 3 or 4 minutes to infuse and cool down a little.

Strain this flavoured milk into the egg mixture, stirring well, then return it all to the pan, which you have just rinsed out. Heat this custard mixture, stirring non-stop, until it boils and thickens – and it *will* thicken, believe me. Reduce the heat and cook gently, stirring all the time, for 2 more minutes, then pour into a buttered 20-cm (8-inch) square tin, spreading it out to a depth of 2.5cm (1 inch). Let it cool, then pop it into the refrigerator to become firm – ideally, it needs a few hours.

Turn out the custard and cut into squares or fingers. To make the coating, beat the egg with the 2 tablespoons water and dip in the custard pieces, then coat them in breadcrumbs. Heat the oil and butter, if using, in a frying pan – you need it to a depth of about 2.5cm (1 inch) – and fry the custard squares, a few at a time, until they're brown, about 4–5 minutes. Remove with a slotted spoon, then sprinkle them with sugar mixed with the cinnamon. Serve hot or cold.

PS If you pour over a spoonful of anis and light with a match, you have *Leche Frita al Anis*.

Pijama

A Spanish version of knickerbocker glory.

For each serving

1 caramel custard, or flan as the Spaniards call it, see page 195
Several scoops of ice cream in different flavours
Lots of fresh fruit – for example, banana, pineapple, peaches, pears, strawberries
A whirl of fresh whipped cream
And, of course, a cherry for the top

Carefully remove the caramel custard from its mould and pop on to a serving plate or into a bowl – or, for that matter, into the bottom of a tall glass. Cover with scoops of ice cream – whatever you like, or whatever you have – chocolate, pistachio, strawberry or vanilla. Pile on some fruit, smother with cream and pop a cherry on top.

Prune Ice Cream with Armagnac

Helado de Ciruela con Armagnac

This is another super pudding that is made commercially in Spain, but is best of all when home-made.

Serves 6–8

1 litre (1¾ pints) vanilla ice cream – see Almond Ice Cream on page 193 if you want to make your own
100g (4oz) stoned prunes, soaked overnight in 125ml (4fl oz) Armagnac
125ml (4fl oz) Armagnac

Take the vanilla ice cream out of the freezer for about 10 or 15 minutes to soften it, otherwise you'll have a problem trying to mix the prunes with a frozen brick.

In the meantime, put the prunes into a small saucepan with their soaking liquid and a little water and simmer gently for 10 minutes. Drain, reserving the liquid, and chop them.

Put the softened ice cream into a large bowl, mix with a wooden spoon for a moment to even out the consistency and fold in the chopped prunes. Pop back into its container and return to the freezer to harden.

Mix the reserved prune juice with the second lot of Armagnac and serve this potent sauce poured over the ice cream.

PS You could try this recipe with dried apricots instead of prunes. Apricots and Armagnac are another dazzling combination.

Almond Ice Cream

Helado de Almendra

This delicious custard-based ice cream gets its wonderful flavour from the Spanish nougat called *turrón*, made from almonds, honey and egg whites. It is made in hard and soft varieties – make sure it is the soft stuff you buy for this recipe.

Serves 8

About 1 litre (1¾ pints) milk – the creamier the better
1 cinnamon stick or vanilla pod – whichever flavour you prefer
Pared zest of 2 lemons
6 egg yolks
275g (10oz) caster sugar
*375g (14oz) soft almond nougat (*turrón*), finely chopped*

Bring the milk very slowly up to boiling point with the cinnamon stick or vanilla pod – one or the other, not both. Pop the pared lemon peel in the pan and let them infuse for about 5 minutes off the heat. This way the milk will absorb the flavours.

Meanwhile, whisk together the egg yolks and caster sugar. Strain the milk and pour it bit by bit into the egg yolks and sugar. Return this to the pan and heat it very gently, stirring all the time until the mixture thickens, using a wooden spoon. Don't expect the mixture to get very thick – it won't. Do be careful not to burn the custard – dark brown burnt bits don't exactly enhance the ice cream. Cool it down completely, then pour it into a suitable container, cover and freeze. When the mixture begins to set after about 2 hours, stir in the chopped nougat, and continue freezing. Then stir again half an hour later – if you don't have an ice cream maker that is – and once again 20 minutes later. Leave in the freezer overnight.

Flan de Huevos con Nata

The puddings in most ordinary Spanish restaurants are mainly bought in from commercial suppliers and, by and large, they are jolly nice. Two typical ones are the famous Spanish *flans*, a common crème caramel-type one, which is made from milk, and one made with cream, which has more the flavour of crème brûlée. But they are even better if you take the trouble to make them yourself. Both recipes follow.

Serves 4

300ml (1/2 pint) single cream
150ml (1/4 pint) milk
1 vanilla pod or 1/2 teaspoon vanilla essence
4 eggs
40g (1 1/2 oz) caster sugar
2–3 tablespoons granulated sugar
150ml (1/4 pint) double cream

Put the single cream and milk into a heavy-based saucepan and heat it very gently with the vanilla pod until it is very hot but not boiling. Turn off the heat and let the mixture infuse for a few minutes. Remove the vanilla pod.

In a large bowl, whisk the eggs with the caster sugar until they are thick and pale. The quickest way to do this is with an electric hand beater. Pour over the flavoured creamy-milk and mix well. Add the vanilla essence here if you didn't use a pod.

Divide the mixture between four small ovenproof dishes and stand them in a roasting pan or similar. Pour hot water into the pan so that it comes halfway up the sides of the dishes. Transfer to a preheated oven, 160°C/325°F (gas mark 3), and cook for about 40 minutes until set (test with a knife to check). When they are done, let them cool down for about 15 minutes.

Next, heat the grill so that it is really hot. Sprinkle the granulated sugar evenly over the tops of the custards and grill them so that the sugar bubbles and caramelises.

Serve with a bowl of whipped double cream. You can eat them hot or chilled.

Flan

Serves 4

100g (4oz) granulated sugar
1 tablespoon cold water
Few drops lemon juice
1 tablespoon boiling water
4 eggs
50g (2oz) caster sugar
450ml (3/4 pint) milk
1 vanilla pod or 1 teaspoon vanilla essence

First of all, make the caramel by putting the granulated sugar in a small heavy-based saucepan with the cold water and the lemon juice. Heat gently, waiting for the sugar to caramelise, shaking the pan carefully from time to time so that you get the sugar to caramelise evenly. It needs to be a really rich golden brown colour – watch that it doesn't burn or else it will taste quite bitter. Turn off the heat and add the tablespoon of boiling water, being careful, as it will splutter. Turn the heat on again and let the caramel dissolve in the water.

Pour this caramel into the base of 1 large serving dish or 4 small moulds or soufflé dishes.

To make the custard, whisk together the eggs and caster sugar. Heat up the milk with the vanilla pod, almost to boiling point, then let it cool and infuse for about 10 minutes. Remove the pod and pour the milk into the egg mixture, beating well. If you didn't use a vanilla pod, add the essence now.

Strain this egg custard into the serving dishes. Pop them into a roasting dish, with enough hot water to come halfway up their sides – a *bain-marie*, in fact. Cook the custards in a preheated, low oven, 150°C/300°F (gas mark 2), for about 1 hour, until they are set. Test with a knife to check – it should come out clean.

Let the custards cool, then run a knife around the edge and invert them. They taste wonderful served at room temperature with some cream that has been warmed slightly.

Santiago Cake

Tarta de Santiago

PHOTOGRAPH OPPOSITE PAGE 169

I am absolutely hopeless at cooking puddings, but I do love eating them. The ubiquitous *Tarta de Santiago* – a beautiful almond-flavoured cake that is eaten as a pudding – is absolutely scrumptious when freshly baked. I was given this recipe by Señor Hernandez, who runs a great restaurant called Casa Peregrino, about 15 miles outside O Grove, on the Galician coast.

Makes 12 slices

3 eggs, size 2
225g (8oz) caster sugar
100g (4oz) butter
175g (6oz) self-raising flour
125ml (4fl oz) water
225g (8oz) ground almonds
Grated zest of 1/2 lemon
Icing sugar } *to decorate*
A few almonds, chopped }

Plop the eggs into your food processor with the sugar, butter, flour and water and whizz together for a minute or so until all the ingredients are well blended. (If you don't have a processor, then I'm afraid you'll have to work quite hard for about 15 minutes beating the ingredients together properly by hand.) Tip in the ground almonds and grated lemon zest and whizz for a few seconds, just to mix. (You don't put the almonds in at the beginning because they would become overworked and oily.)

When everything is mixed, tip it all out into a lined, well-greased, 20-cm (8-inch) cake tin. Level the surface and bake in a preheated oven, 180°C/350°F (gas mark 4), for about 1 hour. Test the cake with a skewer to make sure it is done – pop it back for longer if needs be.

Cool the cake in the tin for 10 minutes, then turn it out and let it cool completely. Dust with some icing sugar and sprinkle some chopped almonds over the top.

Sponge Cake with Nuts and Cherries

Bizcocho Esponjoso con Nueces y Cerezas

PHOTOGRAPH OPPOSITE PAGE 169

Makes 12–16 slices, depending on how greedy you are

150g (5oz) butter or margarine
Finely grated zest of 1 lemon
150g (5oz) caster sugar
225g (8oz) self-raising flour
Pinch of salt
3 eggs, beaten
50g (2oz) pine nuts or flaked almonds
50g (2oz) glacé cherries, rinsed and chopped
12 sugar lumps, roughly crushed

Cream together the butter or margarine with the lemon zest and caster sugar until the mixture is really light and fluffy. You can employ your hand-mixer to do the job instead, if you prefer. Sift together the flour and salt. Beat the eggs into the creamed mixture gradually, adding a little flour as you go along to prevent the mixture from curdling.

Fold in the rest of the flour with a metal spoon, then turn this mixture into a greased and lined 23-cm (9-inch) cake tin. Level the surface, then sprinkle the nuts and cherries on the top. Scatter over the crushed sugar, then pop the cake into a preheated oven, 180°C/350°F (gas mark 4), for about 35–40 minutes, until it is cooked. (Check with a fine skewer to make sure – if it comes out clean, then the cake is ready.)

Let the cake cool in the tin for 15 minutes, then turn it out and allow it to cool completely before you demolish it.

Churros

Churros are delightful little confections of light batter, deep-fried, sometimes dredged in sugar and sometimes eaten with salt as a savoury niblet. They are like a very, very light doughnut, only they are not, and are similar to the *beignets* you find in France. They are popular at breakfast time, dipped into coffee or chocolate, and they are also found on street stalls at *fiestas*. They do not keep well and should be eaten at once.

Serves 4

250ml (8fl oz) water
5 tablespoons oil
½ teaspoon salt
200g (7oz) plain flour
Vegetable oil for frying
Icing or caster sugar for dredging
½ teaspoon finely grated lemon zest
½ teaspoon ground cinnamon

Put the water, oil and salt into a small saucepan and bring up to the boil. While it is heating up, measure out the flour, because as soon as the water is boiling you have to shoot the flour into the pan, all at once, beating it in with a wooden spoon to make a smooth, stiff ball of paste.

Let the paste cool down a little, then put it into a large piping bag, fitted with a star nozzle. Pipe out strips about 10cm (4 inches) in length or make loop shapes instead. Heat the oil – it must be a minimum of 2cm (¾ inch) deep and fry about four at a time, bearing in mind that they swell as they cook. When they are golden brown, remove them from the pan with a slotted spoon and drain on kitchen paper.

Dust the *churros* in a mix of the icing or caster sugar with the lemon zest and cinnamon while they are still hot, and eat at once.

Chestnut Nougat

Turrón de Castañas

The Spanish are keen on sweet, sticky things and here is a delicious one that you can eat with your morning coffee or after dinner.

Makes about 10 servings

450g (1lb) chestnuts, washed
75g (3oz) unsalted butter, melted
75g (3oz) plain chocolate, grated
75g (3oz) vanilla sugar (or 75g/3oz caster sugar flavoured with 1/4 teaspoon vanilla essence)

In a good-sized saucepan, cover the chestnuts with water and bring up to the boil (leave their skins on, but nick them first with a sharp knife). Reduce the heat and simmer gently for about an hour, until the chestnuts are tender. Allow them to cool for a while and, when you can handle them comfortably, peel off their shells and skins, making sure you remove the inner skins as well.

Press them at once through a fine sieve – it somehow works better when they are still warm. Alternatively, you could use one of those mouli-graters to grind them really finely. Put them into a bowl with the melted butter, grated chocolate and vanilla sugar and mix well with a wooden spoon.

Turn the mixture into a cake tin, smooth the surface and put the tin in a cool place for about 24 hours so that the mixture sets.

After a few hours, use a sharp knife to mark it out into bars. When the 24 hours are up, separate these bars and wrap them in greaseproof paper. Store in the refrigerator and eat within a week.

Agua de Valencia

All the English bar and restaurant owners in Benidorm look like retired football managers with good if slightly flamboyant haircuts and plenty of gold jewellery. But they are a cheerful, friendly lot, and though it may sound a bit naff, it is great sometimes to have a bacon sandwich made with Mother's Pride bread imported from England, or baked beans on toast.

I spent a terrific morning in a pub called the Magic Roundabout, a haven for Brits, because it pays lip-service to Spanish food but really comes on strong with steak and kidney pies and all those good British favourites. They also had rugby on satellite television so that in between takes I was able to sit and watch the games. And while I was watching and chatting to the manager Terry Williams we drank this rather innocuous-sounding but lethal drinkette.

Makes about 1 litre (1¾ pints)

Ice cubes
Orange juice – freshly squeezed is best
1 bottle of cava, *Spanish sparkling wine*
Cointreau

Make this potent little number by putting a couple of handfuls of ice into as large a jug as you can find. Pour over plenty of fresh orange juice and then add the bottle of bubbly. Let the fizz subside a bit, then add the magic ingredient – Cointreau. Now I know how the pub where we tried this, the Magic Roundabout in Benidorm, got its name.

Sangría

There are many variations but the basic recipe is made with red wine, brandy, cinnamon, bits of fruit and some fizz (for example, fizzy orange, lemon or soda). If you want to make it stronger add more hard alcohol. Make sure it is served icy cold – allow plenty of time for it to chill in the refrigerator.

Makes about 1 litre ($1^3/_4$ pints)

1 lemon, thinly sliced
1 orange, thinly sliced
1 apple, diced
1 pear, diced
Banana liqueur
Cointreau
Brandy (we used Spanish brandy 103 – it should be quite a light one)
1 bottle of dry, full-bodied red wine (we used Viña Chiringuito)
1 small bottle of fizzy orange, chilled
1 small bottle of fizzy lemon, chilled
1 teaspoon sugar
1 cinnamon stick
Ice cubes

Put the lemon and orange slices with the diced apple and pear into as large a jug as you can find. Then add a generous amount of the banana liqueur, Cointreau and brandy. Pour in the bottle of wine and leave to chill thoroughly. When the drink is really cold, pour in the fizzy orange and lemon and add the sugar and cinnamon stick. Throw in a few ice cubes, pour into some glasses and drink it.

Queimada – An extremely potent flaming brew

Despite its inauspicious start, my dinner with the President of Galicia (see page 49) was a great success and, before he shot off, cloaked by security guards, to wield his mysterious and mighty powers, Señor Iribarne made Queimada, a very special Galician drink surrounded by ritual and superstition. A drink to invoke friendly spirits to bring us good fortune and happiness. In the darkened room he set fire to this potent brew, which flamed eerily as he incanted ancient Spanish and Celtic verses.

I don't know about spirits in the heavens, but there were definitely plenty in this flaming cauldron and it certainly put dear Pritchard in a happy frame of mind. As for me, with a severely upset stomach, I just had to abstain and grin and bear it.

Makes enough for rounding off a party, or getting it going

1kg (2½lb) granulated sugar
4–5 bottles of aguardiente *(or Italian* grappa *or French* marc*)*
Finely grated zest of 1 lemon

You may find *aguardiente* called *orujo* too. It is a powerful Spanish liqueur whose name literally means 'hot water'. After the grapes have been pressed, their skins are put into huge pots with water and boiled. The distilled liquid – the *aguardiente* – is the basis for this wonderful hot drink, which was introduced by the Arabs and is served in mugs.

First, acquire a huge shallow earthenware casserole dish that is flameproof. Tip in two-thirds of the sugar and pour in all the liqueur, stirring well, then add the lemon zest. Bubble for at least 20 minutes.

Take a tablespoon of the reserved sugar in a large serving spoon. This spoon is going to get hot, so arm yourself with an oven glove. Now fill the rest of the bowl of the spoon with liquor from the pot. Strike a light and set fire to the spoon, holding it over the casserole. Wait until the sugar in the spoon starts to bubble and caramelise, then lower it into the pot, which will ignite. Repeat with two or three more spoonfuls of sugar. Ladle into some small earthenware mugs.

PS As an alternative, you can also add orange zest, a few wedges of apple or some coffee granules.

SOME NOTES ON INGREDIENTS AND EQUIPMENT

AGUARDIENTE DE ORUJO is an explosive spirit made, like the French *marc*, by distilling the grape skins or pips left over from fermentation. The Galicians use it to make *Queimada*, see page 202.

ANIS This aniseed-flavoured liqueur is water-white and comes in both sweet and dry varieties. It is drunk chilled or over ice and is popular in cooking.

ARTICHOKES, GLOBE The flower bud of the thistle-like artichoke plant, the globe artichoke should have stiff, tightly-packed leaves. If the leaves have opened out, the artichoke is growing into the flower and becoming old and tough, so avoid choosing these. The leaves should be green, showing no brown patches or tips.

The edible parts of the artichoke are the bases of the leaves, which you nibble when cooked, and dip into some garlicky mayonnaise, hollandaise sauce or melted butter. The other delicious bit is the artichoke heart, which lies underneath the inedible 'hairy' choke.

The Spaniards prefer young, small artichokes, which are more tender than those usually sold in Britain. Whichever you buy, you must first wash them well, taking off any discoloured leaves. Break off the stalks, leaving about 2.5 cm (1 inch) attached to the artichoke. Using a small sharp knife, slice about 2.5 cm (1 inch) off the conical top horizontally, and discard. To remove the hairy choke, either cut the artichoke in half, exposing the inner lining of the heart and scrape away the choke, then throw away. Alternatively, pull out the purple short inner leaves from the top collar of leaves and scrape away the hairy choke, being careful not to remove the heart. Artichokes discolour quickly and should be rubbed with lemon juice as soon as they are prepared.

Boil the artichokes in a huge pan of simmering, salted water for 30–40 minutes, until the outside leaves can be easily pulled away. Artichoke hearts are available in cans from delicatessens.

CAZUELAS Spanish cooks favour earthenware cooking pots. These wide, shallow vessels – glazed on the inside and unglazed on the outside – are useful because they heat up evenly and then retain the heat for quite some time.

If you are fearful that the *cazuela* will crack when you use it on top of the stove as Spanish cooks do, then just use it as a casserole dish. Alternatively, you could treat it to prevent it from cracking by half filling the pot with water, adding about 2 wineglasses of vinegar and boiling these together until the liquid has evaporated. Even so, avoid rapid temperature changes when using the *cazuela*.

CHORIZO These peppery garlic-flavoured Spanish sausages feature in several of the recipes in the book. They are great in many of the wonderful, soupy stews.

Many varieties exist from different parts of Spain, but all have two ingredients in common: paprika, which gives them their unmistakable colour, and pork, though this can be combined with other minced meats. Some types are for slicing and eating raw while others are for cooking. Italian delicatessens are a good place to find *chorizo*. Be careful of bastardised versions that are poor imitations of the real *chorizo*, which should be short, stubby and paprika-red.

MORCILLA This Spanish dark-coloured blood sausage is a relation of our own black pudding. Apart from pigs' blood, it contains onion and sometimes rice, cinnamon and pine nuts. It is soft in texture and is often used alongside *chorizo*. If you cannot obtain *morcilla* you could use good-quality Scottish or Lancashire black pudding; otherwise, just leave it out of the recipe altogether.

OLIVE OIL Butter is rarely used in Spanish cooking and though you can use olive oil from any country in the recipes, do not substitute a different type of oil if you want to achieve any degree of authenticity. Although some connoisseurs believe that the best olive oils come from Italy and the South of France, the robust, fruity, aromatic oils of Spain can be very fine indeed.

Choose whether you want a strong-tasting oil from the first pressing, virgin olive oil, which is preferable for salad dressings, mayonnaise, soup and meat dishes, or a milder oil from the last pressing, usually called 'light' or semi-fine, which is good for sautéeing and fish recipes.

PEPPERS These are one of the great vegetables of Spain. Red and yellow ones are more mature and sweeter than green ones. Choose medium peppers for stuffing, small, slim ones for frying whole, and plump, fleshy ones for grilling. Peppers are best in mid- to late summer when in peak season.

One flavour of Spanish cooking that is difficult to reproduce is the concentrated, earthy taste of the dried sweet red pepper, known as the *ñora*, *pimiento romesco* or *pimiento choriceros*, which are hard to obtain outside Spain. If you bring some back, soak them in cold water for an hour, remove the seeds and scrape the flesh off the skin, then use.

RIOJA WINES Rioja country is a highland area around Logroño in north central Spain, not far from the French border or indeed from Bordeaux. The region has plenty of rain and long springs and autumns so its wines are less hearty than those from other parts of Spain. It is divided into three districts: Rioja Alta (lightest and best wines); Rioja Alavesa (stronger); and Rioja Baja (more alcoholic and cheaper). When phylloxera devastated the French vineyards in the 1870s many winegrowers moved south to Spain. After phylloxera swept there too, they returned home leaving their methods of producing wine behind. Riojas are still made as Bordeaux was in the nineteenth century; they are aged several years in oak barrels (two or three for ordinary wine, up to ten for *reservas*), which gives them a tawny colour and a soft vanilla flavour that comes from the oak. With some of the less reputable producers this effect was achieved by the addition of oak essence. In recent years this practice has been clamped down on and this together with a shift of public taste has resulted in a lighter style of wine being produced. Some of the top producers, though, are once again ageing the wine in the best-quality oak barrels.

SAFFRON The most expensive of all spices, saffron is distinctive in flavour, and a little goes a long way. When adding to a dish that has plenty of liquid, just crumble the threads lightly and put straight into the pan. For drier dishes it should be infused in a little hot water or other liquid.

SERRANO HAM (*Jamón Serrano*) Spanish raw ham is deservedly famous. The best *serrano* ham comes from the black or red Iberian pig, which roams the mountains semi-wild. The finest hams are cured for several months in the cool air of mountainous regions, hence their name of mountain hams. Mass-produced hams are now available, but these are left to cure for a matter of weeks rather than months.

Serrano ham is widely available in delicatessens but its nearest substitute would be Italian *prosciutto* or Parma ham. If you want the ham as a *tapa*, ask for it thinly sliced. If using it for cooking, buy it more thickly sliced so that you can dice it for the pot; the dish will then benefit from both the flavour and texture.

SHERRY The sherry district of Spain surrounds the beautiful old city of Jerez de la Frontera, not far from Cádiz. The old Arabic name for Jerez was Scheris and its anglicised version, sherry, has become famous as the fine wine. Sherry is made from the Palomino grape and matured by the complex *solera* system, a traditional method of fractional blending. Owing to the presence of a natural yeast, called *flor*, which contributes to the process of maturation of the wine and to the alcoholic content, the same must produces four styles of sherry:

fino the driest of sherries. It develops beneath a film of oatmeal-white *flor*, which protects it from the air and keeps it pale in colour.

manzanillas are the pale, crisp and dry *finos* that come only from Sanlúcar de Barrameda in the sherry district. They are reputed to obtain their distinctive 'salty' flavour from Sanlúcar's sea air.

amontillado these grow out of *fino* sherry and are amber yellow with a dry, nutty flavour. After *fino* has been in the barrel for six years, the *flor* dies and falls to the bottom of the cask so the wine comes into contact with the air.

oloroso grows little or no *flor* and is the darkest, richest and softest of sherries. *Olorosos* develop in contact with the air and may attain alcohol levels of 24°.

SNAILS In Spain and many other Mediterranean countries gathering snails after a shower of rain is a favourite pastime. The snails are then starved for a few days to rid them of poisonous herbs or pesticides. But by far and away the best way is to opt for cultivated snails that have been cleaned and ready-prepared.

SQUID These are usually sold whole by weight, though you can sometimes buy squid 'rings' – the sliced body pouch. Your fishmonger may prepare the squid for you.

If not, first cut off the tentacles and set aside. Gently pull off their heads and discard, along with the eyes, innards and ink sac – unless using the ink for the recipe on page 68. Take out the quill, which looks like a piece of transparent plastic, from the body pouch and wash away all the white fluid. You should now be left with the body pouch or 'hood', which has two triangular fins, and the tentacles. At the base of the tentacles is the 'beak' or mouthpiece – take it out and discard.

The hood or pouch can be stuffed or sliced into rings, or it can be cut into squares and scored with a diamond pattern to tenderise it. The tentacles are usually sliced and cooked.

WINES See also Rioja and Sherry. Spain has more land under vine than any other country, yet only produces one-third of Italy's, the world's largest producer, output. Very simply, the country may be broadly divided into three main wine-producing areas: the north for the best table wines such as Rioja and Penedès in Catalonia; the hotter central zone for bulk wines with high alcohol; and the south for *vinos generosos*, apéritifs like sherry and dessert wines. *Cava* wines are sparkling wines from Catalonia made according to the Champagne method.

INDEX

INDEX